LOST FOR WORDS

DYSLEXIA AT SECOND-LEVEL AND BEYOND

A PRACTICAL GUIDE FOR PARENTS AND TEACHERS

WYN MCCORMACK

First Edition published l998
Revised 2002
© Wyn McCormack 2002

ISBN 0 9532427 14

Cover Design   Michael Lunt
Printed by   ColourBooks Ltd., Baldoyle, Dublin 13
Published by   Tower Press, 3 Priory Drive, Stillorgan, Co. Dublin
Typeset by   Carole Lynch

In memory of Tom,
who gave me the encouragement
and confidence to write this book.

Table of Contents

Glossary of Terminology

CAO   Central applications system for Universities, Nursing, Institutes of Technology and other colleges.

CERT   State agency for training in the hotel, catering and tourism industry.

DAI   Dyslexia Association of Ireland.

DIT   Dublin Institute of Technology comprising the College of Commerce, Aungier Street; Colleges of Technology, Kevin Street and Bolton Street; College of Marketing and Design, Mountjoy Square, College of Catering, Cathal Brugha Street and the College of Music.

ESRI   Economic and Social Research Institute.

FETAC   Further Educational and Training Awards Council which gives accreditation to Post Leaving Certificate courses.

HETAC   Higher Education and Training Awards Council which gives accreditation to national degree, diploma and certificate courses in the Institutes of Technology and other colleges.

IATI   Institute of Accounting Technicians of Ireland.

LCAP   Leaving Certificate Applied Programme.

LCVP   Leaving Certificate Vocational Programme.

NEPS   National Educational Psychological Service.

NCI   National College of Ireland.

NUI	National University of Ireland, comprising of UCD, University College, Dublin, UCC, University College, Cork, UCG, University College, Galway, St. Patrick's College, Maynooth.
NCAD	National College of Art and Design.
PLC	Post Leaving Certificate Courses.
UCAS	Centralised application system for degree and diploma courses in the U.K.

Introduction **1**

The origins of this book lie in the journey of discovery I have taken since 1985 when it was confirmed that our twin sons, Robin and Simon, had a learning difficulty. It was a journey that began in ignorance. In spite of the fact that I was a secondary teacher, I knew little about the subject of dyslexia at that time. Although I received help from teachers, psychologists and DAI, (the Dyslexia Association of Ireland), it was a journey taken for the most part on my own as I tried, over the years, to assess what exactly were the twins' difficulties, what techniques worked best for them and what resources were available to them. In recent years I have met with parents soon after a child was similarly diagnosed and have heard the same questions being asked and have seen these parents starting out on the same path searching for the same information.

My primary objective in writing this book is a hope that it will be a source of relevant and practical information for parents of children with dyslexia.

At the time the twins were diagnosed, I was fortunate in that I was working as a guidance counsellor, as indeed, I still am. My role as a guidance counsellor put me in a central place in the school system where I have access to information relevant to their needs. I deal with the vocational, educational, and personal counselling needs of students from the ages of twelve to eighteen. I am involved, among other things, as a member of a team looking after the needs of students with diverse learning difficulties. I receive copies of psychological reports on such students. In cases where students appear to have learning difficulties, I suggest referral for educational psychological assessment to their parents. I keep up-to-date with the trends in employment and educational courses available after second-level. This is a rapidly changing field with more flexibility entering into the routes to qualifications. This flexibility can be particularly important for students with dyslexia. Up to 2001 I also was a subject teacher of Business and English. However since then my teaching hours have been allocated to the new role of resource teaching. During the years my roles, as a teacher, a guidance counsellor and more recently as a resource teacher, have been of great benefit to the twins and the corollary of this is that I have become much more aware of dyslexia and the difficulties that students with dyslexia face in second-level education. These difficulties are shared by students with other hidden learning difficulties such as Dyspraxia, Asperger's Syndrome and Attention Deficit Disorder.

A second objective in writing this book is to increase the awareness of the needs of such students in the public mind and, in particular, the teaching profession. While there has been some progress in recent years, much more is needed. I have personally known many students who were not diagnosed until their mid-teens. They had passed through primary school and partially through second-level without teachers picking up their difficulties and advising an assessment. Certainly they have met with failure and their confidence and self-esteem have been affected greatly by such a late diagnosis. It is my belief that there are many such students with undiagnosed learning difficulties in Irish schools.

During much of the time that I have been involved with DAI, campaigning as a member of the Association for more resources and more teacher training on the topic of learning difficulties, very little changed. This was reflected in the first edition of this book in 1998. However since then there have been developments which hopefully will lead to better provision for students with learning difficulties in Irish education. These include the establishment of the National Educational Psychological Service, the Report of the Task Force on Dyslexia, the Education Act 1998, the Education (Welfare) Act 2000 and the Equal Status Act 2000.

I will be referring to the twins, Robin and Simon, and the techniques which worked for them and some that did not throughout this book, so it may be helpful to give a brief introduction to them, our family history and to explain how the dyslexia has affected them.

They were our first children and were already showing some signs of difficulty at the age of two. They were slow to talk. We attributed some of this to 'Twintalk', which is that they were so busy communicating between themselves that it slowed down their language development. At a later stage they mispronounced words. They also found sequences difficult to remember and they tended to be clumsy. They did not tie shoelaces until they were nine and they rode a bicycle for the first time at the age of ten. In their early years at school they found order and pattern difficult and they repeated a year. As they had started school at four years and ten months, this made them old for their class.

On the basis of a psychological assessment, we were fortunate to get places in St. Oliver Plunkett's School in Monkstown when they were eight. St. Oliver Plunkett's is a primary school which was established to provide specialised tuition for pupils who have reading difficulties. The twins spent two years there. They went back into fourth class in Carysfort National School but, since their reading was still three to four years behind, they had considerable difficulties with the primary school curriculum. We applied for and received an exemption from Irish from the Department of Education and Science. This helped. It had been hard to see them struggling to learn the sounds in English and then having to learn different sounds for the same letters in Irish. During the years in Carysfort they attended the DAI Saturday morning classes and also attended summer school. It is much to their credit that they tackled all this extra work with perseverance. Towards the end of their years in primary school, their reading developed and this opened the way to making progress in school.

After much research about second-level schools, we decided to send them to St. Gerard's, Bray, for their secondary schooling. Here, provided they received help at home with notes for the different subjects, they coped well. As this was one of the early years of the Junior Certificate course, there were no revision handbooks available, so it was a question of summarising the books ourselves. For the first time they were participating fully in class and received great affirmation when they passed class exams and tests.

They continued to need help with notes during the three years of the Junior Certificate course and also needed help with goal-setting and organisation of work. They attended the examination preparation classes run by the DAI. They both were delighted to receive three honours grades on honours papers in the Junior Certificate and good passes in their other subjects. This gave an enormous boost to their confidence and it showed how far they had journeyed since learning to read at the age of eleven.

They sat their Leaving Certificate in 1998. They took their subjects at Ordinary level. Their results were mainly B's, with one 'A' and inevitably both received a 'D' in English. Robin went to the National College of Ireland to study for a National Certificate in Computing. This was much more suited to his abilities than the Leaving Certificate which has so much verbal content. He achieved a Merit grade and proceeded on to Dundalk Institute of Technology to do a National Diploma. He is now working in the computer industry. Simon has completed the Accounting Technician qualification with IATI and is now working in the Civil Service.

They still have difficulties with spelling. I can never see them spelling well but they use a word-processor with a spell-check competently.

During these years my husband, Tom, and myself decided early on that I was more suited to work with the twins as I am a teacher. Part of the reason I was able to work with the boys is their co-operative and pleasant personalities and their desire to achieve. Together we formed a very compatible work team (for the most part). At times progress was infuriatingly slow; at times impatience set in. I learnt to recognise when, as a result of being too tired, I became more edgy and far more critical. A difficulty which might have been laughed at in September could be the basis for a row in February when we were much more fatigued. I learnt to deliberately avoid confronting issues when under stress. To give out about schoolwork on some occasions would be detrimental to the other work we had put in on self-esteem and confidence. We wanted Robin and Simon to feel home was a refuge and that our love was not conditional on school performance.

Together as a family we have shared moments of great exhilaration and satisfaction at their achievements, such as their Junior and Leaving Certificate results, doing An Gaisce Awards at bronze and silver level, their participation in the Young Scientist Competition and of course, when they both graduated from their chosen courses at third-level.

Because there was a gap of six years between the twins and their brother Tom, it meant we were able to give them more attention than might be possible in a family situation where the siblings are closer together in age. It also meant they had very little competition inside the family. In some families it can increase pressure on the student with dyslexia when younger brothers and sisters overtake their achievements in school tasks such as reading and writing. Soon after Tom died in infancy, the youngest member of the family, Ted, was born in 1986. He is minimally affected by dyslexia. We were conscious of the fact that dyslexia can run in families and had become aware of adult members in the family who have dyslexic characteristics. From the beginning we had been on the look-out for indicators that Ted might be dyslexic but because he was a very articulate, logical child with good co-ordination, we had felt there was no problem.

However, by first class, we discovered he was memorising the content of his readers, so it appeared as though he could read but in reality he had no grasp of reading. He was assessed by a psychologist and his results showed an uneven profile of ability with exceptional strengths in the logical and mathematical areas, average ability in verbal skills and below average in spelling. He received intensive remedial intervention and it had dramatic effects. His reading is now well above average and he is making good progress in school. There is a residual spelling difficulty and learning Irish and other languages remains hard work. He is a good example of how early intervention can minimise the effects of dyslexia in some students.

During these years we have spent many hundreds of pounds, if not thousands of pounds, on the three boys. Assessments and extra tuition are major costs. We received no financial help from the State. This experience is mirrored by many families who had to fund the necessary assessments and tuition costs. These were the fortunate students. There are many cases where families do not have the necessary resources to help the child.

We realise we have been fortunate in benefiting from the support services which were provided by the Department of Education and Science. Robin and Simon received on-going remedial help in school; they went to St. Oliver Plunkett's School in Monkstown for two years; they received an exemption from Irish from fourth class on and they had reasonable accommodation in state examinations. Not all students with dyslexia have the same access to such facilities. Because they did the Leaving Certificate in 1998, their certificate does not have an explanatory note stating they did not participate in some element of the exam. Such an explanatory note is put on the results of students who avail of reasonable accommodation in state exams since 2000.

Over the years we have received great help. Between the three boys they have attended the following schools and colleges:

◆ Mount Anville National School, Kilmacud.
◆ St. Oliver Plunkett's School, Monkstown.
◆ Carysfort National School, Blackrock.
◆ Scoil San Treasa, Mount Merrion.
◆ St. Gerard's School, Bray.
◆ National College of Ireland.
◆ Dundalk Institute of Technology.
◆ Dun Laoghaire Senior College.
◆ Institute of Accounting Technicians of Ireland.

The staffs of all these institutions have always been most co-operative and positive and have done their utmost to meet the boys' needs. They have listened and tried to facilitate our requests. Our thanks to all the teachers concerned. In particular thanks are due to the Headmaster and staff of St. Gerard's School. The twins had six years of second-level education there and Ted has followed in their footsteps.

DAI has been an invaluable source of information. The newsletters and lectures have helped us to understand dyslexia, how it affects students and how to help them cope. I have attended their lectures and conferences. Over the years the twins have attended their Saturday School and exam preparation classes. Parents of children with learning difficulties should become members of this organisation. It is a great support to talk to other parents of dyslexic students, to share information and to feel that one is not struggling alone.

My colleagues in St. David's Secondary School, Greystones, have given me great advice and instructed me in their own particular subjects so that I could help with the twins' homework, as well as listening and giving me constant encouragement.

Much thanks are due to two friends, Pamela McAree, who did trojan work editing this manuscript and my colleague, Cairbre O Ciardha, who gave me advice and suggestions.

I hope that my book will pass on some of the insights I have gained and that it will help students with dyslexia, their parents and their teachers to understand how dyslexia can affect students at second-level and what can be done to help them overcome their difficulties. I also hope that it might raise public awareness. If teachers, parents and the general public are more aware that such problems exist, it will lead to earlier identification and to more facilities and support systems being provided.

Dyslexia at Second-Level and Beyond

2

My knowledge about dyslexia results from my own practical experience as a teacher, a guidance counsellor and, most important of all, a parent. From the time my husband and I became aware that Robin and Simon had a learning difficulty, I have read many books and attended courses to further my knowledge. So when I describe dyslexia it is with knowledge gleaned from the books I have read, from seminars I have attended and from practical experience in the school and at home.

While I try to give an overall description of dyslexia, I am looking in particular at the way dyslexia can affect a student at second-level and beyond. This is the sector of education in which I work and have experience.

Dyslexia is diagnosed by an educational psychologist who identifies marked under-achievement in language skills in comparison with a student's level of intelligence. The word itself comes from the Greek meaning 'difficulty with words or language'. International figures show it occurs in about 4% to 8% of the population in varying degrees and with varying effects. As yet reported figures are far lower in Ireland (see Chapter 7). As dyslexia is a very imprecise term, the term Specific Learning Difficulty is also used. This term reflects the fact that the range of dyslexic characteristics is so diverse and dyslexic students may not suffer from the same characteristics or to the same extent. The profile of the student's strengths and weaknesses is unique and specific to that student.

In 1991 research by Pumfrey and Reason in the U.K. showed that 87% of psychologists preferred the term 'Specific Learning Difficulty' and only 30% thought the word dyslexia useful. My own opinion favoured this term originally. However there has been a widening of the meaning of the phrase 'learning difficulty', with the growth of kinder or more politically correct terms for educationally handicapped children. The precise meaning of the term is often not clear. At least the public have some concept of what the word dyslexia means.

Pollock & Waller in their book *Day-to-day Dyslexia in the Classroom* refer to the fact that in the United States the term 'learning disabled' is used. This can be shortened to LD which is beginning to be accepted as 'learning different'. This is a far more positive term. It takes into account that every one of us has learning difficulties in some form or another. Some people can be excellent readers but have difficulty in Maths or in understanding machines. The student with dyslexia is unfortunate in that his learning difficulties are centred on skills that are so critical to school achievement and where it is so obvious when a child fails.

Since more boys than girls appear to be affected by dyslexia, to improve the flow of the text, I refer to the student as a 'he' throughout in preference to the more clumsy he/she. Of course, all I say refers equally to girls.

Dyslexia is not related to low intelligence. Generally it is true to say that intelligence and reading ability are strongly linked. Students with dyslexia are different. Intelligence and language skills are not correlated for them. There are plenty of cases of students with very high IQ scores who had difficulty in written language skills. Some of the historical figures of which this was true are Einstein, Edison, Yeats, Leonardo Da Vinci and Rodin.

While psychologists are not sure as to the causes of dyslexia, there is evidence of a genetic component. In March 1996 I attended the AGM of the Dyslexia Association of Ireland, at which Mr. T. Pottage from the British Dyslexia Association spoke on the advantages of computers for dyslexics. Mr. Pottage, who has a dyslexic son, made the comment that dyslexia is often inherited. Parents inherit it from their children! It is only since his son was diagnosed that he has recognised some of the effects of dyslexia in himself. The same is true of myself. I had no difficulties at school and went on to third-level education. However now I recognise that I do have some difficulties. I can never tell right from left and I transpose letters and numbers. My own family history would lend itself to the argument that there is a genetic component in dyslexia. My brother was diagnosed as dyslexic in his mid-teens and my three sons are all affected to some extent. Robin and Simon would lend even stronger evidence to a genetic component. They are identical twins and, in their difficulties with languages, have mirrored each other. At the time they were learning to read, they made exactly the same mistakes. 'Saw' became 'was' and 'on' became 'no' for both of them. Even now, when writing, they make similar spelling mistakes. If there is a history of dyslexia in a family, parents should be on the look-out for indicators that a child may be affected. The earlier the child gets help, the less the damage to self-esteem.

Happily there are now screening tests which can point to possible problems for the child from the age of four. These became available from 1996. The DEST (Dyslexia Early Screening Test) and DST (Dyslexia Screening Test) have been developed at the University of Sheffield and trials of these tests have been held by the Psychology Department in Trinity College, Dublin. The DST is designed for use with students from 6 years and 6 months to the age of 16 years and 5 months. The tests are available from ETC Consult.

CoPS (Cognitive Profiling System) is a computer based test to screen for dyslexic characteristics in the four to six age group. It was developed at the University of Hull. It measures the child's reaction to various challenges on a computer screen. It has been updated and now has four programmes:

- CoPSbaseline for children between four and five and six months
- LucidCoPS for children between four and eight
- LASS Junior for children between eight and eleven
- LASS Secondary for children between eleven and fifteen

Up until the development of these screening tests, the earliest a child would be assessed was at age seven or eight. The reason for the assessment would be worries over the child's achievement in school. The child would already be failing. If screening tests can point to dyslexia at the age of four or five, before the child has fallen behind, help can be given earlier and the difficulty may not become so acute. Importantly, if a child has to wait until seven or eight to be diagnosed and is already falling behind, his self-esteem is already being affected. This compounds the difficulties for the child. Afraid of appearing to fail they can become experts in avoiding tasks that they do badly. Evasion tactics used can be psychosomatic illnesses, acting up, tantrums or becoming the class clown. They can give up trying, as it can be preferable to fail by not working at a subject rather than by not being able to do it. This is particularly relevant at second-level when the peer group is so important to the developing adolescent.

THE PSYCHOLOGICAL ASSESSMENT

Parents and/or teachers may voice concerns about a child's progress. Such concerns may be confirmed by the use of screening tests. However, to be able to make a positive diagnosis of dyslexia, it is necessary to have a psycho-educational assessment carried out by a suitably qualified psychologist. Such an assessment may be carried out through the school by a National Educational Psychological Service (NEPS) psychologist, or parents may opt for a private assessment. Even for privately arranged assessments there may be a waiting list of several months. For parents who want to arrange a private assessment, DAI carry out such assessments or the school may recommend psychologists who have previously assessed students. The Department of Education website (www.education.ie and then under NEPS) has a list of approved psychologists' names. This list was published as part of a scheme that allowed schools to purchase private assessments if NEPS do not provide a service to the school. The cost of a private assessment is tax deductible and can be claimed on the MED 1 tax form.

The assessment involving tests and observations lasts over two hours. There may be some brief oral feedback immediately after the assessment, but a report of the assessment will issue some time later. This is a detailed and important document. It will contain the following information:

- Name and address of student, date of birth, chronological age and date of assessment.
- Reasons for referral.
- A note of the tests used and results obtained. This explains the child's abilities and weaknesses, and comments on the child's coping strategies.
- Background information on the child such as developmental history, medical history and family history.
- Recommendations on the type of help, teaching strategies and support services the child needs.

A main component of the testing is an intelligence test such as the Wechsler Intelligence Scale for children, 3rd edition (WISC 111) which contains the following sub-tests.

Verbal (tests given and answered orally)

- Information: General Knowledge
- Similarities: Ability to form concepts and think abstractly
- Arithmetic: Simple problems in mental arithmetic
- Vocabulary: Understanding and explaining words
- Comprehension: Understanding of the everyday world
- Digit Span: Attention to the spoken word, a test of short-term auditory memory.

Performance (tests given by looking, writing, or manipulating pictures)

- Picture completion: Powers of observation
- Picture arrangement: Involves logical sequencing ability
- Object Design: Ability to perceive detail
- Block Design: Spatial Reasoning
- Coding: Speed in writing and copying abstract symbols

When scoring the test, the child's age is taken into account. A score for each test is calculated ranging from 0 – 20, the average for each test being 10. The scores are added up and statistically converted to give a verbal IQ score and a performance IQ score. A full-scale IQ score is arrived by combining both the verbal and performance scores and converting them. The profile of a student with dyslexia on sub-tests of the WISC can show significant differences, indicating the child's strengths and weaknesses. Dr. Hornsby in her book *Overcoming Dyslexia* says 'Very significant clues for the diagnosis of dyslexia are the low scores on Digit Span and Coding tests. These indicate a lack of short-term memory for abstract symbols, shapes and numbers'.

Other diagnostic tests could include tests of laterality and tests of visual and auditory memory, such as digit span, immediate visual recall, recall of designs, and fine motor and ocular motor control.

The report is an important document. It can be used by parents to help them understand the child's difficulties and to make informed educational choices. Because parents are the main decision-makers for the student, I have been surprised to discover occasions where they did not have access to a copy of the psychological report. Teachers should use it to work out teaching strategies for the child, based the child's strengths and weaknesses. Parents and/or primary level schools should ensure copies of all assessments are sent to the second-level school prior to the student entering 1st year. In the case of students receiving additional resource teaching at primary level, the second-level school needs the assessment in January prior to entrance as the requests for such additional teaching hours are made to the Department of Education and Science in February. The report may be used when applying for additional teaching help, exemptions from Irish or the third language requirement in NUI, support services at third-level, the use of assistive technology or reasonable accommodation in state exams. A recent report, usually under two years old, is generally required for such applications.

DYSLEXIA AT SECOND-LEVEL

By the time students arrive at secondary school at the age of twelve approximately, most students with dyslexia are able to read to some extent. If they have been lucky enough to be diagnosed early, they may have received some remedial/resource teaching. Some may have attended DAI workshops or have had extra tuition on a one-to-one basis. Indeed, if students cannot read by this stage, they will have major and serious problems managing the second-level curriculum.

Many people believe that dyslexia is a problem with reading and that, if the student learns to read, the problem is solved. However it must be remembered the huge variety in the range and extent of the difficulties experienced by students with dyslexia. Each student has his own unique profile of strengths and weaknesses. At second-level, students may experience difficulty in one or some of the following:

Reading

Most students with dyslexia will be able to read by the time they reach second-level. However the reading may be laboured or be affected by pressure of time or complicated texts. They can be slow at reading and can misread some words. They possibly confuse letters and sequences. They can concentrate so much on deciphering the text that they can lose comprehension. They may have to re-read a page to make sense of it. It can take them longer than other students to find a word or passage on a page. Even if they can read quite fluently, they may dislike reading aloud. In the pressure of an exam a student with dyslexia, who can read quite well, is quite liable to misread a question as stress can exacerbate dyslexic symptoms.

When students start at second-level their textbooks can be quite daunting. The texts are usually geared for the three years of the Junior Certificate course and many of the texts use the language suitable for students of fourteen or fifteen. This does not help students with dyslexia. They may find it difficult to pick out the main points and summarise the material in the textbooks. This skill is critical to success at second-level where students have to be familiar with so much information. Effective study technique requires students to be able to take notes of key points. They may also have difficulty when using reference material in picking out the relevant points they need and so become flooded with information.

Spelling

Whereas most students with dyslexia will have achieved some level of reading skills by the time of entry to second-level, spelling difficulties tend to persist for a longer period. Students with dyslexia may not perceive the sequences or patterns that letters make to form words. They can lack the visual memory of words. Many people spell well because they remember the visual shape of a word. They become aware if the word "looks" wrong. Students with dyslexia may not have this memory. Typical errors include:

- transposing letters, e.g. hostipal for hospital
- letter confusion, d/b, p/q and m/w being mistaken for each other
- omission of letters or endings e.g. spraind for sprained
- phonetic spelling, e.g. kawphy for coffee, barax for barracks
- impossible combinations of letters e.g. qiet
- inconsistent spelling where the same word is spelt several ways
- adding or deleting syllables or vowels, e.g. rember for remember

If they take the time to try to spell correctly, it can slow down the writing process and interfere with the flow of ideas. Sometimes they try to avoid a word they cannot spell and seek an alternative. This can sound stilted and interrupt the flow of language. Some may mispronounce words and this can have dire consequences for spelling.

Handwriting

Handwriting can be difficult to read and badly formed. This may be the result of directional confusion and/or poor motor visual skills. Directional confusion affects concepts such as up/down, left/right, top/bottom. The student, when beginning to learn to write, does not know which way the pen should go. A video produced by the Eagle Hill School, Connecticut, tries to give parents, teachers and psychologists some insight into the difficulties faced by the student. There is an exercise to illustrate directional confusion. A mirror is set on a desk and a person is asked to copy a pattern but can look only into the reversed image on the mirror. Try this one out yourself and it will give you some appreciation of how difficult some students find the task of orientation. Another way to experience this is to turn the mouse of the computer upside down and to try to move the cursor on the screen. This may seem an extreme example. However when I first began to use the mouse, this is what I experienced for about a week until I learnt to make it an automatic task.

Note-taking

Many students with dyslexia face difficulties in taking notes either from the blackboard or in a lecture. Poor motor visual skills mean they find it difficult to combine looking at the board, copying into their notebook and then looking up to find the right place to continue. Visual memory problems mean they may take fewer words down from the board each time and so are looking back to the board more often. The writing on the board is likely to be in script handwriting which they may have difficulty deciphering.

In a lecture students with dyslexia may have to concentrate fully on what is being said in order to understand it. It is as though they have to translate it to make sense of it. The direct connection where a student can take down what a lecturer is saying and write simultaneously may not apply. This slows them down. If faced with words they cannot visualise and so cannot spell, they can come to a halt and so miss whatever is said next. Besides the problems of taking down notes, the finished copy is likely to be difficult to read and to study from because of poor handwriting and misspellings.

Presentation of Work

Their work can be difficult to correct because of poor handwriting, poor or bizarre spelling and lack of layout on the page. Spacing of work, margins and headings do not come naturally to some students with dyslexia. They can lose marks because teachers cannot decipher what they have written. It can also take far longer to correct. Teachers can sometimes judge students on the appearance of their work. If the work is very untidy and disorganised, assumptions may be made about the content with the consequence of lower marks.

Verbal expression

Some students with dyslexia have difficulty retrieving the correct name for a familiar object from memory. They know all about the object and what it does but the recall of the exact term eludes them. They may resort to terms like 'you know what I mean' or 'thingamijig'. When learning history, they may know the causes, course and results of an historical event such as the Reformation but the names of the people, events and places do not come to mind quickly. When attempting to explain something at length, they can lack organisation and structure. They may know what they want to say but they do not start with a beginning, go on to a middle and thence to a conclusion. It can be very mixed up.

Written Expression

While students with dyslexia may be familiar with a topic and have plenty of ideas, their written answers may lack planning and structure, so the points they wish to make are not clearly represented. Writing can be a cumbersome task and one which students may wish to avoid. Answers may be far too short and points may be left undeveloped. Sentence construction and punctuation can cause difficulties in clarity and precision of writing.

Sequencing

Sequencing plays a part in some of the other difficulties listed in this section. However it deserves to be mentioned separately because sequencing information is so important at second-level. Poor sequential skills may affect a student in the following ways:

◆ He may not perceive the day-to-day sequences that most people take for granted such as the days of the week or the months of the year. This can make planning homework and revision difficult. The teacher may feel he has communicated clearly his instructions to the class but the student with dyslexia does not share the same concept of the time scale and so misinterprets what the teacher has said. The structure of each day at second-level is not the same. The student may forget to do homework or take books in to school on the correct day.

◆ If the student is given a task of learning a sequence off-by-heart such as poetry or spellings, he may find it virtually impossible as he will confuse the sequence. With a lot of effort, it might be learnt in the evening, but is forgotten by the following morning. For this reason some students may find it difficult to tell jokes. They can mix-up the punchline and ruin the joke. If this happens with jokes, how much more difficult is it to learn a long poem?

◆ When given a question either orally or in writing, he may find it difficult to sequence his answer. This can mean that although he may know a lot of information, he cannot find the means to express it in a clearly structured way.

Maths

In Maths students with dyslexia may have difficulty in remembering sequences such as tables which can slow down calculations or the sequence of the steps to be followed in a long question. They may also take longer to distinguish between symbols such as +, -, and < >. They may not grasp the distinction between words with exact meanings such as minus, subtraction and reduction. Small link words, which the student may overlook, can change the meaning of an instruction leaving the student confused, e.g. six <u>by</u> six, six <u>times</u> six, six <u>into</u> six, six sixes, six <u>plus</u> six and six <u>and</u> six. In a verbally expressed question it can be the English in the question and not the mathematical concept that they do not understand. In Maths the student usually works from right to left, which is opposite to the way words are read. This can add to the difficulties. Poor layout and presentation can mean answers are wrong even if the method is correct. In an oral test the student may need to decode the question to understand what he is being asked to do and so he misses the next question and falls behind. One student described a tables test at primary level by saying 'by the time I saw the numbers in my mind, and wrote the answer, I had missed the next question'. This student needed time to visualise the question.

Directional Confusion

This has been mentioned under handwriting but it can affect students with dyslexia in other aspects of the school curriculum. They may find it difficult to tell left from right, read maps, have difficulty finding their way about and remembering routes. In Physical Education or in other subjects where they have to follow a certain action, they may have to translate the action into instructions in their mind as to what their limbs should do. They do not automatically know which arm or leg to use. Frequently the teacher teaches by example. If the teacher is facing the students, when doing an action, it can confuse the student because it is the mirror image of what the student should do.

Following Instructions

The student with dyslexia may have difficulty following verbal instructions if more than one instruction is given at a time, particularly if direction or sequences are included. If the teacher gives an instruction such as 'When you have finished your work, and taken down your homework from the board, you may leave', the student may register the last phrase and leave immediately. This can get him into trouble in school.

Orally given details of school events may lack some essential detail by the time it reaches home and parents. An example may be the notice about a Parents' Night Meeting. By the time it reaches home, the date or the time or the venue may have been forgotten or confused.

Lack of Confidence

The student with dyslexia may experience a few or many of the difficulties mentioned above. However a very common by-product of having dyslexia is lack of confidence or low self-esteem. The student has experienced failure from an early age in a very public arena. He is aware that he does not make the same progress as his peers. It can make him reluctant to ask questions in class. He tries to avoid answering questions in case the answer he gives is wrong. Reading aloud can be embarrassing. He has faced frustration in not being able to do tasks set by the teacher. Being in a classroom may be a source of anxiety and tension to him. He may avoid new challenges so as to avoid further failure. He can lack the confidence in his ability to achieve. He may give up trying. He may be embarrassed by his problem and be reluctant to tell other students that he is dyslexic. Under stress, such as in an exam, dyslexic characteristics can be exacerbated and tasks, previously managed well, become more difficult. This lack of confidence can permeate the whole of his schooling and spread wider to affect sports, hobbies, social relationships and career. This is the most damaging side effect of dyslexia in my opinion.

Again it must be stressed that each student with dyslexia is affected in varying ways. Some may have reading and spelling problems, for others it may be sequencing and structure. Some may be affected minimally, others severely. Teachers and school authorities need to know the profile of the individual student. The psychological assessment gives valuable information and suggestions. Parents should be consulted and listened to. They have the inside track on the difficulties faced by the student and ideas on what strategies work best in the effort to help him achieve his potential.

ALTERNATIVE THERAPIES

In the booklet *All children learn differently, a guide to dyslexia* published by DAI, the Association advocates direct teaching as the optimum way of improving literacy skills. Teaching is time-consuming and often tedious, but when intervention in the form of appropriate teaching begins early in life and has the moral and practical support of home and school, it is successful. The Dyslexia Association's years of experience and knowledge of dyslexia has led it to the conclusion that there is no quick fix, no magic pill, no universal panacea which will provide a cure.

There have been many therapies put forward that claim to cure, prevent or have a positive effect on learning difficulties. Parents and professionals should watch out for any promoted method or product that costs a lot of money and promises an easy or quick 'cure'. Any method or product should be considered controversial and suspect if

- ◆ There is no research to prove it works.
- ◆ The research has not been independently replicated.
- ◆ The claims of the method or product far exceed the research results.

◆ The only proof is the personal testimony of parents or their children.

Before signing any contract, agreeing to any treatment or purchasing any product that sound too good to be true, ask to see the independent research papers that support the claims made on behalf of the product. Also ask professionals in the field about the method.

The Task Force on Dyslexia recommended that the Department of Education and Science commission a review of existing research on the effectiveness of such therapies and interventions.

Some non-teaching strategies for children with dyslexia include:

◆ **Brain Gym.** This is part of the **Educational Kinesiology process.** Kinesiology is the science of body movement and the relationships of muscles and posture to brain function. Further information is available from the Educational Kinesiology Foundation, 12 Golders Rise, Hendon, London NW4 2HR. Website: www.brainwise.co.uk

◆ **Neuro-Physiological Theory** and **Primary Movement Theory** hold that learning difficulties can be caused by primitive reflexes remaining active in the body. Attainment of balance, hand-eye co-ordination, motor control and perceptual skills may be delayed or inhibited as a result. This condition, it is said, may be corrected by a programme of exercises designed to inhibit the primary reflexes. Further information is available from:

The Institute of Neuro-Developmental Therapists, Greenlea Clinic 118 Greenlea Road, Dublin 6. Website: www.inpp.org.uk
The Primary Movement, PO Box 49, Belfast, Northern Ireland. Website: www.primarymovement.org

◆ **Scotopic Sensitivity Syndrome.** Irlen lenses (tinted glasses) have been developed for people with light sensitivity to reduce or eliminate glare which causes some readers to experience perceptual difficulties. Further information from:

Mary Davies, Irlen Clinic, Monkstown, Co. Cork or Marita McGready, 14 Chalet Gardens, Lucan, Co. Dublin.

◆ **Nutrition.** There is a theory that a metabolic problem associated with essential fatty acid deficiencies plays a role in the origin of specific learning difficulties. Its proponents, in particular, B.J.Stordy, point to several studies that show that many children with dyslexia have a shortage of long chain polyunsaturated fatty acids in their tissue membranes. There are commercial products such as Efalex available which supply these fatty acids.

Some parents fear that when the student knows he has dyslexia, the label will encourage him to do less as he has an excuse for not learning. I do not agree with this view. Many students feel a sense of relief. The diagnosis of dyslexia explains their lack of achievement in school and it can encourage them to make an effort provided the tasks are geared to their abilities. One student voiced his relief that there was 'nothing wrong in his head'. Another student was not diagnosed until he was fifteen. Up to this point he had been extremely disruptive and it was very likely he would be asked not to return to senior cycle. Once the diagnosis was made, he changed remarkably. He not only passed his Leaving Certificate, but also was in the running to be considered for Student of the Year at the end of his final year in the school.

There is research to show the dyslexic profile of abilities can contain strengths. Many of these students may be strong in logical reasoning which may lead to success in mastering computers. They may be good at constructional tasks such as building Lego or Meccano. Spatial Relations (the ability to visualise in three dimensions) can be a strength. In a video on dyslexia produced for the BBC programme QED, Tom West, an author who has written several books on dyslexia, suggests that dyslexia is a very positive asset in today's and tomorrow's world and that very good visual spatial relations skills may be more appropriate to a new world rather than the old skills based on words. Humdrum tasks such as spelling and sums can be left to computers. These were the skills of the medieval monks. Tom West has written a book called *In the Mind's Eye* which profiles a number of gifted individuals such as Faraday and Einstein, all of whom had some literacy or numeracy difficulties during their school career and later as adults.

Developments Since 1998

3

I became interested in the provision of services for students with dyslexia around 1988 when the twins were assessed for the first time. The lack of services for students with dyslexia at all levels of education was very apparent. Very little progress was made for a very long time. Key difficulties included: a lack of teacher training both pre-service and in-career; a scarcity of educational psychologists, and poor levels of identification and assessment of children with dyslexia. The Dyslexia Association of Ireland campaigned vigorously over these years with little success. However since 1998 there have been many welcome development which include:

- The Education Act 1998
- The Equal Status Act 2000
- The Report of the Task Force on Dyslexia
- Establishment of the National Educational Psychological Service (NEPS)
- The Education (Welfare) Act 2000
- The proposed Education (Disability) Act
- Increased expenditure on special needs
- Changes in NUI entry requirements

One of the key changes is the recognition of the rights of children to an appropriate education. This underpins many of the new developments. In the past many parents were very much alone when trying to help their child. Requests for assessment often came from parents and not from teachers. Parents had to pay for private assessments. They then often had to find out about whatever help existed and pay for private tuition. The Dyslexia Association of Ireland was founded by parents, who recognising that there was no other help available, began setting up workshops to provide specialised teaching. These activities have expanded and continued to the present day. DAI also set up in-service courses on dyslexia for teachers. Parents who were members of DAI frequently sought to provide primary and post primary schools with information about dyslexia and appropriate support services. DAI have also run international conferences to bring information on the latest research and developments in the field to Ireland and the Association continues to lobby the Department of Education and Science for better services for children and adults.

If the student with difficulties is quiet and well-behaved, it is easier to survive in the school system. However some students with dyslexia become frustrated and this may lead to discipline difficulties. There are also students in the educational system with other learning difficulties such as ADD/ADHD who may have behavioural problems. In the past parents were very much alone when coping with such children. Frequently they were asked to remove the child from school. Frequent long suspensions may have been used as a way to persuade a parent to remove a child. The parents could then find that they could not get the child into another school. Some of these children left education for good in their early teens. This had major implications for their future as it affected their education, career prospects and personal confidence. Some had not achieved adequate literacy skills to be able to read and write. The ESRI in its publication 'Issues in the Employment of Early School Leavers' described the employment prospects for such students as 'low pay, low skill, and frequently temporary' and many young people entering the labour market 'do not have the skills or resources to maintain any long-term position in it'.

Even if the child did not have discipline difficulties, some schools did not want to enrol students with learning difficulties. I have met with several parents who have been told that the ethos in a particular school was academic and so it did not cater for students with learning difficulties. When one considers that up to 10% of the population may be affected to some extent by dyslexia, and that students with dyslexia can come from all abilities levels, such a stance appears highly elitist.

In the past many parents were often left alone trying to make provision for their child. The thrust of much of the new legislation and reports is that schools have a responsibility to provide for the needs of the child. The Education Act 1998 and the Equal Status Act 2000 set out the requirement for the school to provide equal access and participation for children with disabilities/special needs. The Education (Welfare) Act 2000 requires the school to support children with difficulties to attend school on a regular basis. This means the schools now share with the parents the responsibility of providing for the child's needs. The Task Force on Dyslexia recommends that both school and parents be involved when deciding on appropriate supports for a student.

If the schools now have greatly increased responsibilities towards students with special needs, they also need resources and funding to enable them to do this. Clearly if a child has major behavioural difficulties, it can lead to disruption in the classroom. This is not fair and equitable to the other pupils in the class. Schools need speedy access to extra resources such as classroom assistants, resource teachers, and psychological services to provide appropriate resources for such students.

At a meeting with the Department of Education and Science in December 2001, the representatives of school managements sought clarification on the resources needed to provide for students with special needs. Schools need the records including assessments and reports to accompany the child on transfer from primary to secondary. All remedial/resource hours and care assistants allocated at primary level should be automatically transferred with those pupils when the move is on to second-level schools. A short-term deficit in assessments exists until NEPS is fully developed in 2004 and this logjam can lead to students losing out on support resources for the critical first and second year period after transfer to second-level.

THE EDUCATION ACT 1998

This Act begins with the statement that it is 'An Act to make provision of the common good for the education of every person in the state including any person with a disability or who has other special educational needs'. It then carries on to describe the rest of the Act. But the importance of special educational needs is recognised by making such a strong opening statement. One of the definitions given to disability is 'any condition or malfunction which results in a person learning differently from a person without the condition or malfunction'. It also states the term 'special educational needs' includes the needs of the exceptionally able student.

The Board of Management in a school should use the resources provided to it to make reasonable provision for students with a disability including alterations to the building and the provision of equipment as long as the provision does not go beyond 'nominal cost'. This is not defined and such a definition may eventually be determined in the courts. The School Plan should state the objectives of the school relating to equality of access and participation and the steps the school proposes to take to achieve these objectives including equality of access and participation by students with a disability or other special educational needs. A grievance procedure is provided for in the Act.

THE EQUAL STATUS ACT 2000

This Act covers discrimination on nine separate grounds such as race and religion. One of these grounds is disability. The Act states that 'educational establishments shall not discriminate in relation to the admission of a student or access or participation of a student on any course'.

TASK FORCE ON DYSLEXIA

In September 2000 the Minister of Education and Science, Dr. M. Woods, set up a Task Force on Dyslexia. Its brief was to review the current range of educational provision and support services available to children with specific reading disabilities in Ireland, to assess the adequacy of current educational provision and support services and to make recommendations for the development of policy approaches, educational provision and support services.

The report was completed in 2001 and published on the Government website at www.education.ie. It is also available from the Government Publications Office. The Task Force looked for submissions from the public and received 399 written submissions. The Task Force also decided to look for oral submissions from the public. This recognised the fact that some individuals with dyslexia would find it easier to make an oral submission than a written one. Adverts quoting a free telephone number were made on the radio. As a result 896 oral submissions were received. The report acknowledges the contribution made by these submissions and took them into account when making recommendations.

The Task Force proposed a definition of dyslexia which recognised the broad range of difficulties which arise from the condition and which also took into account recent research findings.

'Dyslexia is manifested in a continuum of specific learning difficulties related to the acquisition of basic skills in reading, spelling and/or writing, such difficulties being unexpected in relation to an individual's other abilities and educational experiences. Dyslexia can be described at the neurological, cognitive and behavioural levels. It is typically characterised by inefficient information processing, including difficulties in phonological processing, working memory, rapid naming and automacity of basic skills. Difficulties in organisation, sequencing, and motor skills may also be present.'

It recognised that the learning difficulties arising from dyslexia:

◆ Occur across the lifespan and may manifest themselves in different ways at different ages.
◆ May co-exist with difficulties in the area of numbers.
◆ May be associated with early spoken language difficulties.
◆ Increase or reduce in severity depending on environmental factors.
◆ Occur in all socio-economic groups.
◆ Co-exist with other learning difficulties such as Attention Deficit Disorder (ADD).

It is a common perception of dyslexia is that it has to do with reading and spelling and so this definition is very useful as it is acknowledges the wide range of difficulties that may be present.

A welcome statement in the report is that 'each student with learning difficulties arising from dyslexia should receive a level of provision appropriate to his/her needs'. The report found the criteria used currently to identify students who need special educational resources is 'problematic'. For one thing, some students are not adequately provided for because they fall marginally outside current eligibility criteria. Priority for learning support is given to the child who scores at or below the 10th percentile on appropriate nationally-normed standardised tests of reading and/or Maths. To access resource teaching support at primary level, the criterion for students with a specific learning difficulty is the child is at or below the 2nd percentile. The Task Force noted that other children may be excluded because of the difficulty in accessing the form of assessment required by the current criteria. The Task Force recommended that since the difficulties presented by students with dyslexia range along a continuum from mild to severe, **there is a need for a continuum of interventions and other services**.

The Task Force suggested a scheme that would involve class teacher, learning support teacher and parent working in co-operation. The role and contribution of parents is emphasised throughout the report.

Altogether the Report made 61 recommendations. If these recommendations are put into effect, the provision of services for students with dyslexia will dramatically change for the better. The Task Force recognised the need for urgent implementation of the recommendations, which were divided into two categories, short-term and medium term. The short-term recommendations should be implemented in the school year 2001/2002 and the medium term within three years. Included in the recommendations are:

- Provision of an independent appeals procedure for parents dissatisfied with the level of provision.
- Referral of the practice of putting explanatory notes on the Certificates of students who avail of reasonable accommodation in state exams to the Director of the Equality Authority.
- Provision of training on the topic in pre-service training courses for teachers.
- Provision of in-career development courses for subject teachers.

◆ Every primary and post-primary school should incorporate into its School Plan a policy for addressing the needs of students with learning difficulties and for involving parents in all aspects of its response to these needs.
◆ The number of places for training of educational psychologists should be increased.
◆ Grants or tax relief should be given to parents for the purchase of assistive technology where such has been recommended.
◆ Advice and information on dyslexia should be freely available in schools to parents and teachers.

It is well worthwhile for parents and teachers to read the full report. There is an executive summary and a summary of the recommendations. These tend to be formally expressed and need to be read carefully to understand their implications. However, throughout the report itself, very practical advice is given. It is here that one can see the influence of the contribution made by parents and students themselves. The everyday language used reflects the voices of the contributors. One section lists practices to be avoided by teachers such as

◆ Asking the student to read aloud in class, unless s/he wishes to do so and s/he has practised in advance.
◆ Asking the student to copy large amounts of material from the blackboard.
◆ Asking a student to rewrite work because of spelling errors.
◆ Penalising a student for not completing tasks within strict time limits.

Such sensible and clear suggestions are invaluable when considering how classroom teachers can help students.

In a welcome development, in May 2002 the Minister of Education and Science, Dr. Ml. Woods, announced new measures to enhance the education of children with dyslexia following on the recommendations of the Task Force. He said, 'It has been estimated in recent studies that between 6.5% and 8.5% of Irish 14 year olds had literacy difficulties that were likely to impede their educational development and life chances. ... I am committed to making further significant progress on the recommendations of the Task Force over as short a period as possible. I am also committed to improving the accommodations made for pupils with dyslexia in the State Examinations.' The measures introduced include:

◆ On-line training for teachers catering for pupils with dyslexia.
◆ The appointment of 10 new Learning Support Trainers.
◆ Reduction of the pupil teaching ratio in special classes for dyslexia from 11:1 to 9:1.

The full implementation of the recommendations of the Task Force will make a huge impact on the educational provision for children with dyslexia.

THE EDUCATION (WELFARE) ACT 2000

This Act safeguards every child's entitlement to an appropriate minimum education. It focuses particularly on causes of absenteeism. Included in its provisions are:

◆ The establishment of the National Educational Welfare Board which is given the lead role in implementing the Act. The Board will deploy educational welfare officers at local level who will promote regular school attendance and prevent absenteeism and early school leaving. These officers will focus in particular on children at risk who are experiencing difficulties in school in order to resolve impediments to their regular attendance. Alternative schooling will be sought for students who have been expelled, suspended or refused admittance to a school.

◆ School managers will adopt a pro-active approach to school attendance by maintaining a register of students, and notifying the educational welfare officer of particular problems in relation to attendance. They should also prepare and implement a school attendance strategy to encourage regular school attendance.

◆ The Act makes specific provision for the continuing education and training of young persons aged 16 and 17 years who leave school early to take up employment.

◆ The central role of parents in providing for their child's education is recognised. Parents should send their children to school on each school day or otherwise ensure they are receiving an appropriate minimum education. If the child is absent, the parents should notify the principal of the school of the reason for the absence.

NATIONAL EDUCATIONAL PSYCHOLOGICAL SERVICE.

In 1965 the Department of Education established its own psychological service and employed three psychologists. The function assigned to these psychologists was the development of the guidance services in the post primary schools. The Psychological Service remained focused almost entirely on the post primary sector until 1990. Many reports in the 1990's recommended the extension of the psychological services. Other bodies such as parent and teacher bodies, the Psychological Society of Ireland, and the trade union, IMPACT, all called for such development. In 1996 a report produced by IMPACT, the union representing the Department of Education psychologists suggested two hundred and fifteen psychologists were needed to provide an adequate service. At the time thirty-seven psychologists were working in the service.

The National Educational Psychological Service was established in 1999 and is an executive agency of the Department of Education and Science. The development plan for NEPS provides for the gradual expansion over a period of years, with the number of psychologists increasing to two hundred. By June 2002 there were approximately one hundred psychologists in post, and the Civil Service Commission were in the process of completing a selection of a further sixty-nine psychologists.

NEPS has been delegated authority to develop and provide an educational psychological service to all students in primary and post-primary schools and in certain other centres supported by the Department. The educational psychologists in NEPS provide assessments and also provide advice on the identification and screening of children who might need to be assessed. Each psychologist is responsible for a number of schools. The school authorities provide names of children who are giving cause for concern and discuss the relative urgency of each case during the psychologist's visit. This allows the psychologist to give early attention to urgent cases. Where cases are less urgent, the psychologist will, as a preliminary measure, act as a consultant to teachers and parents, and offer advice about educational and behavioural plans and monitor progress. The psychologist is also involved in assessing students for reasonable accommodation in state examinations and in reviewing applications for additional resource teaching hours for special needs students.

There is a backlog of assessment work to be dealt with. Until NEPS reaches the full planned staffing of two hundred psychologists, it is likely that this will continue.

To alleviate the difficulty the following initiatives have been introduced:

◆ The Minister of Education and Science allocated £1.25 million to NEPS for the purchase of assessments from private practitioners. Details on the Department of Education and Science website: www.education.ie

◆ Tax relief was introduced on the fees paid on private assessments. This is claimed by using the MED 1 form.

PROPOSED EDUCATION (DISABILITY) BILL

In December 2001 the Government approved the proposals for an Education (Disability) Bill which will provide a statutory guarantee of education services for people with a disability. It will address the individual needs of children with disabilities in a concerted and comprehensive way. It provides for the following:

◆ A register of children with special needs.

◆ Education plans tailored to the disabilities and educational needs of each individual.

◆ Involvement by parents in the planning and on-going review of their children's education.

◆ Mediation and Appeals structures.

◆ The setting up of the National Council for Special Education as a dedicated statutory body with the responsibility of ensuring that the aims of the Act are met.

◆ Statutory responsibilities on health boards to provide assistance and services necessary for the education of children with special needs.

INCREASED SPENDING ON SPECIAL NEEDS EDUCATION

Expenditure on Special Needs Education increased tenfold in the three year period between 1998 and 2001. It went from £7 million to £70 million. The Minister of Education outlined where this additional spending occurred when addressing the Annual Conference of Learning Support Teachers in 2002. By 2002 there were 1,000 full-time resource teachers for children with special needs in primary schools in comparison with 100 in 1998. Over 9,000 hours of part-time resource teaching took place each week. There were 2,840 special needs assistants to assist with the education of children with special needs. In 1998 there had been only 299. There were close to 200 psychologists employed in NEPS, compared with 44 three years previously.

Building on the investment under Schools IT 2000, the Government in 2001 made a further investment to enhance significantly Information and Communication Technologies in Irish Education. One of the specific objectives and strategies of the new plan is provision for special needs students. It provides for additional grants for equipment for students and teachers. The National Centre for Technology in Education (NCTE) provides support and guidance for teachers of pupils with special needs. Through its publications and website it provides up-to-date guidance and assistance on the purchase and best educational use of equipment.

In 2001 a pilot scheme to assist second-level students with dyslexia was introduced in thirty-one schools. Students with dyslexia in 2nd year in these schools were provided with a laptop for school and home use. This scheme recognised that assistive technology can help students to work more independently.

Such an increase in expenditure on Special Needs means there is more support available for students.

CHANGES IN THE ENTRY REQUIREMENTS FOR THE NUI COLLEGES

The National University of Ireland comprises of the colleges of UCC, UCD, UCG and Maynooth. The entry requirements for these Colleges specify that a student must have six subjects in the Leaving Certificate, two at Higher level, and that the student must include English, Irish and a third language. Since 1998 students with serious dyslexia have been able to apply for an exemption from the third language requirement. The extract from the Matriculation Regulations is included as Appendix C. In the period 1998 to 2001, approximately one hundred applications for an exemption from the third language on the grounds of dyslexia were made, and all were granted. The term 'serious dyslexia' is vague. Does it mean a certain percentile on the assessment tests? Or does it mean that the dyslexia has to have serious consequences for the individual? Why should it not apply to all students with a diagnosis of dyslexia made by an educational psychologist who find achievement in languages difficult?

If the student has an exemption from Irish granted by the Department of Education and Science, this exemption is recognised by NUI. Full details of this are given in the NUI Matriculation Regulations handbook.

In 2001 NUI also stated that

- ◆ It is prepared to consider applications for matriculation from students who, because of exceptional circumstances, do not satisfy the normal matriculation requirements. Such applications are considered on an individual basis and should be accompanied by a School Record Form completed by the Head of school attended and, where appropriate, relevant professional certification.
- ◆ A student who has been allowed an exemption from the study of Irish at school, on the basis of specific learning difficulty, will qualify for exemption from the NUI Irish language and third language requirement for matriculation.

The first statement allows students with diverse learning difficulties, to apply for an exemption from parts of Matriculation Requirements, if it is appropriate for their needs. The second statement means that if the student has an exemption from Irish from the Department of Education and Science on the grounds of specific learning difficulty, they qualify for an exemption from the third language requirement.

Mr. J. Nolan, Registrar, NUI, stated in a letter on 31/8/01 the 'NUI is not aware of students seeking exemption from a third language who have applied for but not been granted an exemption from Irish at school. **However the University is willing to consider any application for exemptions from Irish, in the general context of its policy on granting exemptions'.** Very few students are eligible for an exemption from Irish from the Department of Education and Science (see Chapter 7). The guideline governing the granting of such an exemption is that the student's skills in English are in the bottom tenth percentile. There are many students with dyslexia do not fall within this category and it is more likely that these are the students aspiring to attend to colleges such as NUI.

A student with dyslexia can apply for an exemption from the third language and in the light of the NUI statement above, also could also apply for an exemption from the Irish requirement to NUI, even though the student is not eligible for a Department of Education and Science exemption. In practical terms what this would mean for the student, if both exemptions were granted, is that he would not have to study a third language for his Leaving Certificate. He would have to continue to study Irish in school but, in the event that he failed Irish in his Leaving Certificate, he would still meet the entry requirements for NUI.

Such exemptions are important for some students with dyslexia as in the competitive points race that exists for courses at CAO level, it is important for a student to be able to maximise points by presenting his six best subjects. A common profile for a student with dyslexia is poor achievement in languages. It is very likely that subjects such as English, Irish and the third language would be at Ordinary level. He may have excellent abilities in other subjects. Without exemptions in the language requirements the student may have to take nine subjects in the Leaving Certificate in order to have six Higher level subjects. This imposes two additional burdens. Firstly nine subjects is an excessive amount and secondly the student has to take language subjects in which he may have to work much harder than other students to achieve a pass mark.

If all the recommendations and provisions contained in the reports and legislation are implemented, students with dyslexia and other learning difficulties will be better catered for in the Irish Educational system in the future.

Choosing a Second-Level School

4

Deciding which second-level school would be the most suitable for a student with dyslexia is a key decision for parents. Some parents may not have a choice since there may be only one school for the area. Other parents have a choice, particularly in city areas.

To make the best choice, the parents of a student with dyslexia need to have as much information as possible about the schools and what they offer. Below are some points to consider when choosing a school. Some of this information will be freely available in school literature. The website www.scoilnet.ie gives access to the websites of schools, as well as information on courses and tips for parents. Some may be available on request from the school. Parents of students already in the school can also be a source of information.

CLASS PLACEMENT

How does the school place students in classes? Most schools have more than one class in each year group. Different ways to place students in classes include:

Mixed ability

The class is made up of students from all ability levels. If a school is taking in one hundred and twenty students, the students are randomly broken into 4 different groups of thirty.

Proponents of mixed ability say that it avoids labelling students as failures because they did not get into a higher class. Placement in a bottom class can have a detrimental effect on self-esteem and motivation, a consequence being that students can give up and stop making an effort to achieve. On the other hand some teachers say it is very difficult to teach mixed ability classes and that better progress is made if the class has the same ability level. This is particularly true when teaching Irish, English and Maths at Junior Certificate level, where there are three levels of examination; higher, ordinary and foundation.

A mixed ability system favours the student with dyslexia. He is in a class where he will benefit from the wide range of ideas and discussions. He may be able to use his strong abilities in the class room, for example in debate or class discussion, while at the same time the teacher knows of his weaker skills.

Setting

This means that instead of an overall assessment incoming students are assessed in an individual subject, e.g. Irish, English or Maths. The students are placed in class on their ability in that subject. A student could be in the top Maths class but in a middle English class. This type of placement takes a lot of school resources because all the classes in a particular subject must be held at the same time. If there are one hundred and twenty students in a year group, a school will need four Maths teachers available at the same time. Setting can be of benefit for a student with dyslexia as it can take into account his strengths. However, if he is placed in a weak English class because of his writing skills, although these skills may benefit from the slower pace set by teachers, he may miss the stimulation and ideas that would be present in a mixed ability class.

Streaming

This is where students are placed in classes by their performance at assessment. In the case of one hundred and twenty students, the first thirty could be in the highest stream, the next thirty in the second stream and so on. The class is together for core subjects, typically Irish, English, Maths, Religion, History and Geography.

Streaming is much criticised for the effect it can have on student morale. It may produce a lower stream mentality which can be anti-achievement.

Students may end up in a lower stream for many reasons. Family problems, lack of support at home for schooling or disruptive behaviour can contribute to poor academic achievement. These problems may spill over into class interactions. In an ideal classroom, the teacher is likely to make more progress if the class is at the same ability level. However, while this may be true of top streams, many other factors such as the problems mentioned above can affect the progress in a weak stream. This is probably the worst scenario for a student with dyslexia with average or above average ability. The entrance assessment is not likely to show his strengths and unless the psychological assessment is taken into account, he can be placed in a class that will improve on basic skills but will not provide the challenge and stimulus he needs and the verbal discussion of which he is capable. He may become bored at the slow pace of the class. In some cases this may result in discipline problems. In a bottom stream class there may be more disaffected and unmotivated students. This can mean that class control can take a larger proportion of the teacher's time with a consequential loss of actual teaching.

However some schools, while still streaming, provide a smaller class size for the lowest stream. This may allow for teachers to provide for the individual needs of each of the students.

There is one very important point about streaming to consider particularly in relation to a student with dyslexia. Take a student who has very weak verbal skills and very good Maths. If the student is placed in a lower stream on account on the poor verbal skills, will it deprive the student of sitting higher level Maths in the Junior Certificate? In some schools this can happen. The student may be placed in a lower stream class and as a consequence will sit ordinary or foundation level Irish, English and Maths in state examinations. If parents are aware that the student has an ability profile with strong Maths, they should check this point at the time the student enters second-level. It is too late to discover the student is taking ordinary level Maths at the end of first year or during second year. The student, by then, will have fallen behind the pace of a higher level Maths class.

Parents should also be aware of the format of the entrance assessment. A reading test will give an indication of the student's ability to read, a spelling test will give an indication of his ability to spell but a Maths test, where the questions are verbally put, may be more a test of the student's ability to understand English rather than Maths and may not give an accurate indication of the student's skills in Maths.

Banding

This is an attempt to merge mixed ability and strict streaming. With 120 students, the top sixty students on assessment would be grouped into one band. Two classes would be formed from this group randomly. The weaker sixty students on assessment would be the second band and again two classes would be formed. It means there is no bottom class. Banding reduces some of the negative effects of streaming.

Overall my opinion is that mixed ability or setting best meets the needs of the student with dyslexia.

SUBJECT CHOICE

Parents of a student with dyslexia face the major decision of subject choice when the student begins second-level. This decision can be far more important for students with learning difficulties than for other students as there may be subjects in which these students will not succeed no matter how hard they try and other subjects in which they can make good progress.

Some schools offer a wide choice of Junior and Leaving Certificate subjects while in other schools the choice is more restricted. The subjects on offer depend on the school's resources and the number of pupils attending the school.

A small number of schools have the structure that in the course of first year the student has classes in all the subjects on offer and the decision about subject choice is made at the end of that year. This allows a more informed decision to be made as the student knows how he has progressed in each subject. More typically the parents and student have to choose subjects when the student is entering second-level.

Students following the Junior Certificate programme in a secondary school must take Irish, English, Maths, History, Geography and CSPE

(Civic, Social and Political Education). Normally they choose three or four additional subjects called options. The most commonly available options are Art, Business Studies, Home Economics, Languages, Metalwork, Materials Technology, Science or Technical Graphics. There are other subjects in the Junior Certificate examination which a small number of pupils take such as Technology, Music, Classical Studies, Environmental/Social Studies and Typewriting.

In some option subjects there can be a limit on the number of places due to teacher availability or a maximum class size restriction. The school will have a system for allocating places to such classes.

For some students with dyslexia option choice may be critical. There may be some subjects they will enjoy and do well in and other subjects in which they will find it difficult to make progress whereas a student not affected by dyslexia may achieve equally well in all subjects. When a student has a number of subjects he enjoys, it can change his whole attitude to school. Parents should ask well in advance how places in option classes are allocated so that they can obtain the most appropriate options. In some cases, because of the importance of the student taking the most appropriate subjects, a case for positive discrimination in allocating option places could be made. It would be helpful if such a suggestion were contained in the student's psychological report.

Most students will take nine or ten subjects in the Junior Certificate. For some students severely affected with dyslexia, this may be a particularly heavy burden. The option structure may provide a way to reduce the number of subjects being taken. This is how it could work. The student will take the core subjects, English, Maths, History, CSPE, Geography and Irish (unless the student is exempt from Irish). The possible option structure offered by a school might be that the student take one subject from each of the following lines, giving him four option subjects.

1. French, Art, Business Studies
2. Science, Business Studies, Home Economics, German
3. Science, Materials Technology, Technical Graphics, Business Studies
4. Art, Science, Home Economics.

The student could take the same subject, such as Science, from two different lines. This would reduce the number of subjects he has to sit in the Junior Certificate and double the amount of teaching he is receiving in that subject. This is an extreme solution. Most students with dyslexia are well able to cope taking all the option subjects and in my experience have actually enjoyed their option subjects far more than their core subjects. However such a reduction of options may be helpful in the case of students who are severely affected by dyslexia and are struggling to achieve literacy.

It is difficult to give general advice on which subjects would suit a student with dyslexia as each student has a different profile of abilities. Here is information about subjects which may help in reaching a decision.

Art

Art is a subject without a written exam at Junior Certificate level. At Leaving Certificate level the paper includes written questions on the History of Art. 75% of the final grade in the Junior Certificate is based on projects which the student completes during the exam year. Because the subject is not verbally based, it can provide a rewarding and stimulating subject to students with dyslexia, many of whom have good visual spatial skills. Indicators for success in the subject would be an interest in art and crafts and good hand-eye co-ordination.

Business Studies

Business Studies is one subject at Junior Certificate and splits into the three separate subjects of Accounting, Economics and Business at Leaving Certificate. It contributes to the student's understanding of the world of business and encourages a positive attitude to enterprise. The course includes both book-keeping and theoretical content. The book-keeping aspect of the course may be attractive to the students with dyslexia who have good computational skills. It would be recommended that the student who intends to take Accountancy at Leaving Certificate level should take Business Studies. It is easier to take up Business and Economics at Leaving Certificate as new subjects.

Home Economics

Home Economics is a subject with a mixture of practical skills and theoretical content. There is a project and a practical cookery examination during the Junior Certificate year, both of which carry marks towards the Junior Certificate exam. It leads on to the subjects of Home Economics Social and Scientific and Home Economics General at Leaving Certificate. Career possibilities include hotel and catering, food science, fashion, interior design and paramedical careers. Indicators for success in this subject are an interest in the subject matter and good dexterity.

Languages

Should the student with dyslexia take a foreign language? This is a key question for parents. The importance of languages is being stressed as Ireland trades increasingly with her EU partners. Also it is widely believed that students need a third language to attend university. This third language requirement applies only to the colleges of NUI. Students with serious dyslexia can apply for an exemption from this requirement. This is discussed in greater detail in Chapter 3.

Some students with dyslexia will never make a success of studying a language and it will become a subject in which they face constant failure. This can have an effect on how they view school. Indicators that the student should not take a foreign language include difficulty in reading and spelling in English, poor achievement in Irish, difficulties remembering the sound of new words and recall of new vocabulary. However the language courses have an increasing oral and aural element, so students with good oral and aural ability may be quite successful in mastering another language. Some schools have an option structure that makes the study of a foreign language obligatory and this may not suit particular students with dyslexia.

Materials Technology (wood)

Materials Technology (wood) consists of practical work, theory and drawing. It aims to train students in the use of tools and materials and to develop self-reliance, initiative and accuracy. The Junior

Certificate exam consists of a written theory examination and a practical project. It is studied at Leaving Certificate level as Construction Studies and is suited to those interested in careers in construction, architecture and engineering. Indicators for success in the subject are: dexterity, an interest in the subject and a practical approach to problem solving.

Metalwork

Metalwork introduces students to the various processes, tools and materials in modern use. It has a practical and theoretical content. The student can gain experience in interpreting drawings, planning a work sequence and carrying out a task. At Leaving Certificate the subject is studied as Engineering and provides a sound and knowledgeable basic grounding for those interested in engineering or technical careers. Indicators for success in the subject are: dexterity, an interest in how things work and a logical approach to problem solving.

Science

Science is taught as one subject at Junior Certificate level but splits into the three separate subjects of Physics, Chemistry and Biology at Leaving Certificate level. It opens the doors to careers in technology, medicine and science. A science subject is a minimum requirement for entry to many third-level courses in these areas. The answers required in the Junior Certificate are factually based with very little essay type answers. This may suit the student with dyslexia. The course includes a large amount of practical laboratory work. Because of the need to be scientifically literate in the modern world, it is advisable for most students to take Science as a subject.

Technical Graphics

In Technical Graphics students are trained in the use of drawing instruments and are given a knowledge of the basic geometrical constructions and their practical applications. This subject leads to the study of Technical Drawing at Leaving Certificate and is suited to those interested in careers in architecture, engineering and other occupations of a technical nature. Indicators for success in the subject are: neatness, good hand-eye co-ordination and a logical approach to problems. Some students with dyslexia excel in visual spatial skills and this subject will suit such students.

The subjects Art, Home Economics, Materials Technology, Business Studies (book-keeping element), Metalwork, Science and Technical Graphics have a practical and theoretical content. As a result the student is learning through doing tasks and developing skills as well as learning the theory content. The skills developed are then tested in the exam. This can mean there is less memorising of large amounts of facts. This reduction in rote memory work as well as the multi-sensory approach can suit the student with dyslexia.

One subject that a small number of students take is Typewriting. It is a skills-based subject. Students with dyslexia should develop keyboard skills as soon as possible. Typewriting provides a subject in which they might be successful and which would equip them with these essential skills.

Irish

The student may be exempt from Irish under the Department of Education and Science Directive. Rule 46 of the Rules and Programme for Secondary Schools allows some students with dyslexia an exemption from Irish. One of the grounds for such an exemption is that it is given to students who function intellectually at average or above average level but have a specific learning difficulty of such a degree of severity that they fail to achieve expected levels of attainment in basic language skills in the mother tongue. The guideline is that the student is in the bottom 10% of achievement on a standardised norm-referenced test of reading or spelling. School authorities must receive a psychological assessment that is less than two years old, and must issue a certificate to the student and forward a copy to the Department of Education and Science. Students, who received an exemption at primary level, may be re-issued with an exemption certificate by their second-level school.

Some students may fall within this guideline at one stage, but with additional tuition, may develop their skills in English.

Therefore at one stage they might qualify for such an exemption and, if tested at a later stage, might not. Students who attend the special reading schools such as Catherine McAuley's School in Baggot St. and St. Oliver Plunkett's School in Monkstown may apply for an exemption when leaving these schools.

If the student qualifies for the exemption at a particular point in time, it would be prudent to actually get the official letter showing this exemption. Parents may decide to let a student, who is exempt, participate in Irish class in order to benefit from the cultural aspects of the subject. They will then have the option further on in the education system to withdraw the student from Irish. This could be very important for some students in senior cycle when they need to target their strongest subjects to order to maximise points for the CAO. The exemption will follow the student through to second-level and further. NUI recognises this exemption and also allows a student with such an exemption to be exempt from the third language requirement for entry to NUI colleges (See Chapter 3).

There are some careers where a certain standard of Irish is required. A 'C' in higher level Irish is necessary for primary teaching. The Gardai require the student to have taken Irish in the Leaving Certificate, but will accept a 'B' in foundation level. It affects a small number of career choices if the student does not study Irish.

Sometimes a teacher at primary level, recognising the child's difficulties, allows the child to do extra English work during the allocated time for Irish. However the official exemption has not been issued. If the student is not studying Irish at primary level, it is very important for a parent to ask the school to obtain the certificate of exemption from the Department of Education and Science. Otherwise the child will be required to study Irish when attending second-level.

If the student is exempt from Irish, there should be provision for this class time to be used constructively such as remedial withdrawal or computer time.

Is Irish part of the entrance assessment? If it is, does it play a part in deciding class placement? If the student has an exemption or has attended one of the specialised reading schools, such as St. Oliver

Plunkett's in Monkstown where the emphasis is on mastery of English, with less emphasis on Irish, is this taken into account in decisions on class placement?

Irish can cause some students with dyslexia particular difficulties. The phonics are different so the child who relies on phonics to read and spell can have difficulty. This would also apply to other languages. As well in Irish the order of the words in the sentence also changes with the verb coming first. Students with sequencing difficulties can find this difficult. Also the beginning of the word can change with prefixes in certain grammatical constructions, so the word may not be found in the dictionary if the student tries to look it up.

The Task Force on Dyslexia recognised the lack of assessment instruments and support materials for students whose first language and/or main language of instruction is Irish and recommended that the Department of Education and Science should commission the development of such materials.

DISCIPLINE

Students with dyslexia tend to be disorganised. They need a clearly organised classroom with clearly given instructions and a sense of order as they may need to concentrate quite hard to interpret their teacher's instructions. Some learn much more from listening attentively than they would from reading from a textbook. They require a well-structured and disciplined atmosphere in which to learn. Such a classroom provides the teacher with time to ensure the student understands what is expected and allows the teacher to check individual work. It also ensures a pleasant and relaxing environment. In a classroom where the teacher has to impose order constantly, the teacher can be more stressed and have less time to give to individual students. The atmosphere is more fraught. The flow of the teacher's input is interrupted because of the need to correct students.

In recent years teachers have observed a greater indiscipline in the classroom. The reasons for this are varied. They include: increased amount of family breakdown, less parenting skills so some parents find it difficult to discipline their children and children with little regard for authority who find it difficult to obey discipline imposed by others. The final sanctions open to schools have been reduced. Expulsion of a pupil is extremely rare. Whatever the reasons, there is no doubt the student's progress will be affected if there is difficulty imposing order on a class group.

Students, who are different in any way, may be picked on by bullies. Students with dyslexia may be considered different and may become victims of such behaviour. Most schools now have strong anti-bullying policies. However school authorities need to be informed if bullying is happening. It is possible to prepare students to meet bullying behaviour by teaching them coping strategies in advance. Giving them an understanding that such behaviour is a reflection of inadequacies on the part of the bully may prevent them feeling that there is something wrong with themselves which attracts bullying. Make sure that, if a situation arises, that they know they should talk to the adults in authority.

TRANSITION YEAR

In some schools transition year is part of the curriculum for all students. In others it is not available and in some it is optional. There can be advantages and disadvantages to a transition year for the student with dyslexia.

The advantages of transition year for the student include:

◆ The student may find it difficult to achieve academically. Transition year gives the opportunity to do projects, to obtain new skills, to research possible careers and to experience different methods of working. It is different from the academic work done for the Junior Certificate and the student may do well with this change of approach. Self-esteem may be fragile in the student, who may have had to come to terms with failure in academic areas in the past. Transition year may give him the opportunity to build up self-esteem. Up to now the class may have judged and assessed fellow-students on academic results. This year will allow other aspects of the personality to show.

◆ It gives time to reflect on the type of CV the student has and how to develop it. Some students will not achieve the academic results to compete for courses where points decide the allocation of places. They may be relying on a good CV to help them at interviews.

◆ Project work will help the student to organise goals, to do research and to meet deadlines. These are skills which many students with dyslexia need to develop. However they may need help and support to do it.

◆ Self-esteem can be enhanced during transition year by
  • Work experience.
  • Learning new skills, such as computer skills, typing and organising projects. If the student does not already use a computer, it is important that he becomes skilled with computers during this year.
  • Contributing to the community. This can be the school community or the wider community. Many transition year programmes include a community element, e.g. fund-raising for charities.
  • Achievements such as the President's Award Scheme (An Gaisce), or sporting exploits all build up self-esteem. The President's Award is particularly suitable as the student chooses four challenges in each of the following; community work, sport, new skills and an adventurous activity. If the student meets his goals, the award is given.

The disadvantages of a transition year for the student include:

◆ The programme for transition year may lack structure in some schools and students may lose the study skills they have learned and find it hard to return to serious study in fifth year.

◆ The student with dyslexia may already be older than his classmates if he has repeated a year at some stage. Taking transition year may mean he is relatively old sitting the Leaving Certificate.

◆ The student may feel somewhat at sea in the unstructured curriculum of transition year. Organising project work and setting goals to achieve long-term objectives may be more difficult for him than for other students.

If the transition year is well planned, it can be of enormous benefit to students. The worry that study skills may be affected because of the lack of a defined programme is offset by the development of skills in handing flexible project-related goals. This adaptability and flexibility needed for such work are skills essential for today's job market and for life.

SIZE OF SCHOOL

Large schools (schools of over 500 pupils) can provide a wider range of subjects. With more choice the student may find subjects which he can do well. Smaller schools will have less subject choice, which can be a disadvantage. On the other hand the smaller school provides an environment where each student is known by all the staff. This can have a beneficial effect on self-esteem and strengthen a feeling of being part of the school community. There may also be smaller classes. There may be less streaming.

CLASS SIZE

It is very much to the student's advantage if class sizes are small. In a small class the teacher has more time to pay individual attention to students. Maximum class size guidelines at second-level are thirty students in academic classes such as English or Maths and twenty-four for practical classes such as Science and Home Economics. In state-funded schools classes tend to be close to these numbers. Some schools try to arrange that the numbers of students in the lowest stream are smaller than in the rest of the classes of the year group. This has been helped in recent years by the allocation of resource teaching hours for special needs pupils. The number of students in classes in private schools can be lower as the private schools have additional funds to employ extra teachers.

SCHOOL ATTITUDE TO LEARNING DIFFICULTIES

Some schools can be very supportive of the needs of students with diverse learning difficulties including dyslexia and have structures in place to assist them. However, in a survey of the members of DAI in 1999, only 26% of parents were satisfied with the help their children received in school and two-thirds believed that teachers were not aware of the needs of students with dyslexia. Remember that at second-level, very few subject teachers have had formal training on the topic of learning difficulties. Hopefully this will change as a result of the recommendations of the Task Force on Dyslexia.

In meeting with the principal of a school for the first time to discuss the needs of the student, it will become apparent whether the school has a supportive attitude or not. This is the time to raise issues such as an exemption from Irish, reasonable accommodation in state exams and support services inside the school. Even if the school principal does not accede to requests, the fact that he/she is willing to discuss such issues, will indicate something about his/her attitude.

The Education Act and the Equal Status Act have huge implications for access to and participation of students with disabilities in schools. In the past many parents who spoke about schools who were unwilling to take students with learning difficulties or schools that did not provide adequate support services. These two Acts have made schools more accountable and provide parents with increased rights.

Parents, if concerned about the attitude of the school to learning difficulties, could use questions from the list below and ask for written answers in reply from the school principal.

- Under the Education Act 1998 the Board of Management is required to publish the school policy on pupils with disabilities. Does the school have such a policy?
- Under the same Act the School Plan should state the measures the school proposes to take to achieve equality of access and participation for students with disabilities. Does the School Plan contain such measures?
- The Act contains a grievance procedure, which provides a mechanism for parents to raise grievances about a lack of support services. How can parents access such a procedure?
- Under the Equal Status Act 2000, educational establishments are prohibited from directly or indirectly discriminating in relation to access and participation. What is the school policy on admissions? What criteria are used?

- Some schools use the term *academic* in describing themselves. This is to suggest that as the school is an academic one, the parent should look for a different school to meet the child's needs. What does this term academic mean? Is the school catering only for those who will go on to 3rd level? What about students with dyslexia who have poor verbal-linguistic abilities and who may not perform well at second-level due to the dominance of languages and verbally-based subjects and yet have the ability to go on to 3rd level in specialist areas? Does the definition of academic apply to a top grouping in an intelligence test? Does it mean the school excludes children with learning difficulties? All of these contravene the principle of equality of access. If such a term is used, ask the principal for a written definition of the term as understood by that particular school.

- Equality of participation means the school should provide the relevant support services to enable a student participate. The Act requires a school to do all that is reasonable to accommodate the needs of a person with a disability, so long as such provision does not go beyond 'nominal cost'. This is not defined in the Act and such a definition may, eventually be determined in the courts. Many of the supports that enable a student with dyslexia to participate fully do not require much finance such as in-career training for teachers, study skills training for students, photocopying notes and provision of information and advice to parents on the topic.

One very immediate way to improve teacher awareness about dyslexia and other learning difficulties is to provide in-service training for existing teachers. Schools are allowed one day for in-service training for the whole staff during the academic year. Parents could, either themselves or through the Parents' Association, request that the school consider holding an in-service day on Special Needs. It is particularly relevant now that the legislation has stressed the role of the school in providing appropriate education for students with special needs.

LEARNING SUPPORT/RESOURCE TEACHING

The student, on entrance to second-level, may still need additional help. Such help can be provided by a learning support teacher or a resource teacher. Are such facilities available? Will the student benefit from them? Further information is included in chapter 7.

LEVELS OF PAPERS IN STATE EXAMINATIONS

The Junior Certificate is the examination that replaced the Intermediate Certificate.

In Irish, English and Maths it provides three levels at which the exam may be taken: higher, ordinary and foundation. Roughly about 40% of the students take the higher paper, 50% take the ordinary and 10% take the foundation. The foundation level has been introduced to facilitate students who would have failed to achieve a pass grade in the Intermediate Certificate. Students, who take the foundation or ordinary level in a subject, normally would not go on to sit the Leaving Certificate in that subject at higher level. Foundation Maths at Junior Certificate is likely to lead on to foundation level Maths at Leaving Certificate. *Foundation level Maths and Irish are not acceptable for entry to many courses and careers.* The vast majority of courses in the Institutes of Technology specify the student must have passed ordinary level Maths as well as ordinary level English or Irish at Leaving Certificate. The decision that a student drop to foundation level Maths may be taken as early as second year at second-level and can have serious career implications later on.

In all other subjects other than English, Irish and Maths in the Junior Certificate there are two levels, higher and ordinary. It is intended that the majority of students would take the higher level paper. The ordinary level paper in these subjects is more the equivalent of the foundation level in Irish, English and Maths. A student who wants to do higher level at Leaving Certificate in a particular subject should be taking a higher level paper for his Junior Certificate.

Does the school teach all levels for the Junior Certificate? If ordinary level or foundation level would be more suitable for a particular child, will there be a class at this level? Will the student be in a mixed class with two or all three levels being taught in the same classroom? This is a more difficult situation for the teacher.

TYPES OF STATE EXAMINATIONS

In recent developments of the state examination system, there are now three distinct Leaving Certificates, the traditional exam based Leaving Certificate Programme, the Leaving Certificate Applied Programme (LCAP) and the Leaving Certificate Vocational Programme. (LCVP). These will be discussed in more detail in Chapter 9.

The Junior Certificate School Programme was introduced in forty-five schools in 1996 for students whose particular needs were not adequately addressed in the broadly based Junior Certificate. In 2001 it was offered in one hundred and eighty four schools. It is hoped this programme will reach out to young people who leave school early without obtaining any qualifications. The programme involves greater student activity and specific goals are set for literacy and numeracy. It is based on the concept that all young people are capable of achieving real success in school, and that they can have a positive experience of education, if the conditions are favourable. It is a way of working within the Junior Certificate which is specially designed to help young people who have had a difficult experience of school. Instead of examination grades, a student profiling system is used to measure achievement. Details of the schools offering this programme are available from the Curriculum Development Unit, Sundrive Road, Dublin 12.

If parents consider that a particular type of state examination programme would suit their child, they should enquire if such a programme is being provided by the school. If the parents are interested in a school which does not offer the LCAP or LCVP, they may consider the option of the student changing school after the Junior Certificate or transition year.

FRIENDS

In some cases the student with learning difficulties may have difficulty making new friends easily. This may be the result of past bullying or low self-esteem. Such a student might have a small number of friends. It will help the transition to second-level if he goes to the same school as his friends.

CO-ED VERSUS SINGLE SEX SCHOOLS

While there has been research which suggests that girls' achievement in co-ed schools may drop, having worked in a co-ed school for many years, I see no advantage in one over the other. However in the case of students with learning difficulties, there are some schools where there is a very competitive ethos either academically or on the sporting field. If the student is not achieving academically and is not participating in the major sport of the school, his self-esteem may be affected. In this case I would choose either a school where there is less emphasis on competitive success or a co-ed school where, because of the wide mix of students, there are many different types of activities offered.

EXTRACURRICULAR ACTIVITIES

I have mentioned that self-esteem can be fragile in students with learning difficulties. They have experienced difficulty and failure with the academic part of the curriculum. However they can achieve success and peer recognition in other areas such as the extra-curricular activities organised by the school. Some schools put on a wide range of activities which can include sports of every type, debating, drama, organising a school bank, camera clubs and social concerns such as Amnesty International. Parents should check and see which activities are available.

However it must be remembered that often it is the student with poor self-esteem who may be reluctant to join in group activities. Information about what is available may not reach home as the student is aware that his parents might encourage him to participate. Parents should become aware of what is available by contacting the school. It is much easier to get a young teenager involved in school activities in First Year than it is later on in school life.

DISTANCE FROM THE HOME TO SCHOOL

Living close to the school can facilitate students' participation in extra-curricular activities. Living at a distance from the school can mean the student misses out on social life and friendships. It is more difficult to participate in many aspects of school life if the student is tied to transport timetables or is relying on parents to provide lifts.

SUMMARY

Several different factors should be considered when choosing a school. There will be no perfect school that will meet all criteria. Parents need to decide on what they consider to be the most important. They should then research the schools in their locality and decide on the school which will best meet their child's needs.

Below is a summary of the points discussed in this chapter. They are not in order of importance as such prioritising will very much depend on the student's strengths and weaknesses, self-esteem, and social skills.

- Class Placement
- Choice of subjects
- Irish
- Discipline
- Transition year
- Size of school
- Size of class
- School attitude to learning difficulties
- Learning Support/ Resource teaching
- Levels of papers in the Junior Certificate
- Leaving Certificate and Junior Certificate Programmes provided
- Friendship
- Co-ed versus single sex schools
- Extra-curricular Activities
- Distance from home to school

Coping with Second-Level: How Parents can Help

5

The change to second-level is a big transition point for all students. The student is moving from having one teacher all day to having several teachers in the course of a day. There is also the introduction of new subjects. There is more emphasis on examinations, both state and school-based. The vast majority of students cope well and are very positive about the move and have settled in well by mid-term. However this transition may bring more pressures for the student with dyslexia. The most obvious change is that at primary-level the student will have had one teacher who knows him and his difficulties well. Now the student may face up to nine different teachers in a day. He needs to be organised to face the different demands of these teachers. The primary school curriculum concentrates on numeracy and literacy. Now new subjects appear and must be mastered. It is expected that basic skills in numeracy and literacy are in place. There is a certain curriculum to be covered in time for the state examinations.

Parental interest is a vital component in a student's progress. However there are some extremes to be avoided. Some parents can set unrealistic goals and push the student to achieve them. Others can appear to be disinterested and avoid involvement with schoolwork, perhaps because they themselves found it difficult when they were at school. It must be remembered that dyslexia may be inherited. Others use the student's difficulties as a reason for not making any academic demands at all. However, consistent parental support, based on a realistic knowledge of the student's ability, is invaluable. I believe it to be the most important factor in the development of the dyslexic student's self-esteem and his ability to cope. The parents' role is essential at the start of second-level, but as the student matures, he should gradually take more responsibility for his progress and should apply the appropriate study skills himself. It is a developing process in which the parental input diminishes as the student achieves a growing independence and mastery of the necessary skills.

The Task Force on Dyslexia recognised that the involvement of parents is central to meeting the needs of children with learning difficulties arising from dyslexia and that the parents of students with such difficulties need support and advice but that they have a major contribution to make in achieving effective outcomes. The contributions that parents can make were listed in the Report as:

- Playing a support role to the learner.
- Protecting the self-esteem of the learner.
- Rewarding effort rather than results.
- Contributing to the multi-disciplinary reviews of the child's progress.
- Following up and reinforcing learning objectives.
- Engaging in activities such as paired reading.
- Providing help with assistive devices.
- Meeting with the child's teachers on a regular basis.
- Becoming involved in after-school activities.

The reason why parental support is so critical at the start of second-level is that it is important the student makes a successful transition from primary school. There is a major challenge in coping with all the new subjects, new teachers and the new structure of the school week. If he does not achieve some level of success, there is a risk that, as a defence mechanism, he may turn off the idea of school. As a result he may become involved in 'messing'. Parents can help him meet the challenge of second-level by using appropriate inter-ventions from the suggestions in this chapter. Computers are not covered in this chapter as their contribution is so important that Chapter 6 is solely devoted to the topic. Certainly not all these suggestions will apply to all students. Also parents need to be consistent and keep involved throughout the school year. Trying to do everything can become very onerous and it is easy then for parental efforts to falter. It is better to do a limited amount thoroughly and maintain the effort throughout the year. Read over the suggestions and take the ideas most appropriate to your child's particular needs.

HOMEWORK

Homework is very important at second-level. It consolidates learning from the classroom. When material is taught in the classroom, the student hears it for the first time. It is important he understands what he is being taught at this stage. This material which he understands in class will be forgotten unless the knowledge is consolidated through homework, either written or learning. It will then be forgotten within a few weeks unless it is revised on a regular basis. A revision programme means it will stay in the mind of the student.

Homework can become a battleground, fraught with difficulties. The student with dyslexia can be quite tired at the end of a day in school more so than his peers because he must concentrate harder and simple tasks can take him longer to do. Homework may also take him a longer time to complete. If the hours needed to do homework are excessive, talk to the teacher. If it is taking the student an hour to do a question that will be allocated half an hour in an exam, the teacher needs to know this. Long hours spent at homework will only exhaust the student further.

ORGANISATION OF HOMEWORK

Homework should be done as early as possible in the evening, when the student still has energy. At the weekends encourage him to do written homework on a Friday night. Some students spend a lot of time 'notting', i.e. spending time not doing the homework while at the same time feeling it hang over them like a cloud. They then feel that homework takes all night because they have been thinking about it all night.

A definite routine will help establish good work practices. Homework should be done at a desk or a table, with the books and any equipment needed near at hand. The student should not study with the television or the radio on. Mobiles should be switched off. Such distractions will interfere with concentration. The student should not be interrupted for telephone calls or callers to the door. An agreement can be made that these calls can be returned when the study time is over.

Many people find it difficult to be organised and tidy but some students with dyslexia find lack of order seriously affects their work. A work area with plenty of shelving space; a desk organiser that has a place for pens, staples, paperclips; a filing routine that puts notes into folders every day; the use of different colour folders for different subjects; a routine for clearing out the schoolbag daily and packing it at night for the following day; a study timetable and calendar on the wall; these are some ideas that will reduce chaos and muddle. They should use the class timetable to check their bag for the next day. With the lack of order that can characterise their work, they are likely to forget important books and completed homework for different subjects, unless they have a checking system. Is their bag neat, or do scraps of dog-eared paper lurk in its depths? These scraps of paper often turn out to be poems given for learning or vital notes which the teacher has supplied. If they get photocopied pages from teachers, it is essential to use a filing system.

Learning work should also be done at a desk. Some students find pacing up and down helps to improve concentration but the student should never resort to lying on a bed. It is all too easy to relax and allow the mind to drift off.

Each school will have its own guidelines for homework. I recommend two hours a night for a first year student five nights a week. This will increase in later years. The two hours will include time for written homework, learning homework and revision. It can be helpful if parents and student talk about the demands of homework in the August prior to entry and set out agreed timetables which specify where and when homework is to be done. This can reduce conflict later. Often the scenario is that in October or November, parents get exasperated with or worried about a student who is doing half an hour of homework and claiming he has no more to do. If parents can refer back to the agreed programme, it will help resolve the conflict. From the student's point of view, he benefits from having clear guidelines on what he should do.

Some students find it very difficult to set goals for homework. Parents should ensure the student keeps a homework notebook. It can help if they list all the classes they have in a particular day and write the homework beside the name of the subject. Some teachers write homework on the blackboard, other teachers call it out. Some homework will be written, some will be oral. All should be entered into the homework notebook. The homework notebook can also be used as a diary and a reminder system for projects and other such tasks. As the student can be disorganised, it is helpful if all the deadlines, exam dates and other events in his life are in one diary.

HANDWRITING AND LAYOUT

With written homework, is it the best the student can do or is it carelessly done? If you think it can be improved, try to set higher standards for him. Ask him to proof-read his answers. Reading the work aloud will help identify omissions, grammar, and spelling problems. Some students may not be able to read their own work because of their poor handwriting, so what chance does the poor teacher have?

If handwriting is particularly bad, the major problems can include:

- The backs of the letters are not aligned but go off in all directions.
- Letters like 'a, d, g, o, b,' are not closed.
- The letters wander above and below the line.
- Letters like m, w, u, v, n, r, are not clearly formed, so they all look the same.

It can help if the student tries to correct one of these problems at a time. Doing this can greatly improve the legibility of the handwriting. Using good quality paper for writing can help as well.

Check the layout of Maths. Are the columns of figures straight? Often in Maths and Business Studies, mistakes are made because the columns of figures are not aligned or figures are illegible.

All this checking may seem very onerous for parents. It is in the beginning but it is by the consistency of the checking that standards improve. Over time, a routine will become established and the student will adopt many of the practices automatically which means the parents' role will reduce.

LEARNING WORK

Many students consider homework to be the written work given by teachers. The teachers will find out if the written work is not done and there may be punishment work given. However it may be possible for the student to avoid doing some of the learning work given since it can be more difficult for teachers to check that this work is done by all students.

I see learning work as the key to success at second-level. It is mainly the work learnt by students that will be tested in the house and state examinations. There are some subjects that are skills-based such as Technical Graphics or the practical element of Home Economics. For most subjects, however, there is a quantity of information to be learnt. The first mistake the student makes is to think learning work is less important than written and to avoid doing it. The next mistake is to think learning or memorising happens by 'reading over' the text several times. This is a very common error. Reading over a chapter of history twice does not mean that it is learnt and that key points will be remembered. The student needs to think about what he is going to learn and set out a clearly defined goal, e.g., 'I will learn the six causes and five effects of river erosion'. He must then use notes or make notes. These notes are then memorised.

It may also help at the end of the study period if parents ask a question or two on the topics covered that night. They do not need to understand the material, just open a page and ask a question based on that page. This technique may be helpful to the student by improving the motivation and quality of study because he knows his work will be checked. Also the actual verbal recitation of what he has learned can reinforce the material learnt and help with verbal expression.

NOTE-TAKING

Discussion of learning brings up the subject of note-taking. The ability to extract key points is a critical skill at second-level. Good notes make learning the text much easier and also can help in formulating answers as the student has a structure around which he can organise his thinking. Students with dyslexia can find note-taking difficult for a number of reasons: poor reading skills, the readability levels of the textbooks, the volume and size of the texts and a lack of ability to summarise.

If they are not good at making their own notes, there are books of revision notes for some subjects. These are invaluable. They provide the key points a student needs to learn. These are available in schoolbook shops, both for Leaving Certificate and Junior Certificate levels for most subjects. At Junior Certificate level, History, Geography, Business Studies and Science are available. It can be extremely useful to obtain these notes at the beginning of junior cycle or senior cycle.

When taking notes from a written text, the student should first think about the purpose of the notes and what information he wants to extract from the text. For any student a mass of closely written pages of notes will make revision more difficult than it should be. A mistake many students make is that their notes are far too long. They lift complete chunks of the text and include virtually everything from the main book. Notes should be short, precise, stressing the main points only. Notes should be a third of the length of the text from which they have been taken, preferably even shorter. Layout and presentation of notes can help all students but in particular some students with dyslexia, who, on account of good visual memory skills, may be able to hold the graphic image of the notes in their mind and work to recall the content of the notes from this image. Here are some ideas to help make notes clearer:

◆ Leave plenty of space, particularly margins
◆ Use alternative lines of the page
◆ Use different colours to highlight names and points to be remembered
◆ Use headings and sub-headings
◆ No need for sentences, just put down the key words
◆ Numbering of relevant points can help their recall
◆ Use of mind maps to show the interrelationships between facts

- Organise notes, so there is an index at the beginning and each page is numbered
- Mnemonics can help recall. An example of a mnemonic from my own school days is

    FATDAD, for the six counties of Northern Ireland, Fermanagh, Antrim, Tyrone, Derry, Armagh, and Down.

The technique of mindmaps can help students make notes and see connections between topics. This can help learning. The CareersWorld website at www.careersworld.com has information on mindmaps. Its content is based on the work of Tony Buzan, the inventor of mindmapping. It shows ways to improve memory, to mindmap and improve study techniques.

Two other websites that may be useful are

- www.skoool.ie. This site has study notes and solutions for the Leaving Certificate and Junior Certificate subjects. Some subjects are presented interactively. It also has career information.
- www.homeworktips.about.com. This site is designed to help students develop a study plan.

The Dyslexia Association of Ireland runs examination preparation classes in Dublin for students taking the Leaving Certificate and Junior Certificate. These courses are very useful. The content includes study skills and English skills. There is a waiting list for places. Contact DAI for further details

TAPES AND VIDEOS

Some students will find it useful if their notes are taped, particularly if their aural memory skills are good. The student is then obtaining the information through the eye and the ear at the same time. It might come down to parents actually taping the notes themselves or perhaps a group of parents sharing the task of taping. It is of more benefit to tape notes rather than the full textbook as it is the key points the student needs to be able to recall.

Tapes and videos can be useful in teaching the English curriculum. In Junior Certificate English the teacher has a wide choice of material. If the choice of novels includes those available on tape, it may be helpful to the student. He can both listen and read at the same time. This will help him recognise unfamiliar words. For some students it is so laborious to decipher a page of text that the storyline is lost. Tapes help to overcome this. Ask the teacher to consider choosing texts which are available on tape. However it is important that the text and the tape mirror each other. There are abridged versions of books available on tape that would not be the same as the written version. In the Leaving Certificate English course, videos and tapes of texts are available. Such aids make the students very familiar with the text, the story and the characters but it does not replace reading the text.

Tapes of novels are a way to widen the student's information and stimulate his imagination. These students often do not read for pleasure. Using tapes of novels gives them access to literature that other students of their age have read. The library service has many tapes available. Long car journeys are a perfect opportunity to use them.

Tapes and videos can also be beneficial in teaching other subjects. Students with dyslexia benefit from multi-sensory teaching. The difficulty is finding tapes and videos relevant to the curriculum of the different subjects. During term time RTE Network 2 have educational programmes on throughout the day. Topics covered include Science, Geography and History.

SPELLING

If spelling is a difficulty, the student should keep a spelling notebook in which he writes any new words he meets in each subject and their meaning. The student then learns these spellings by heart. It is often the new words or names that the student will find difficult to recall. The revision of the vocabulary notebook just prior to an exam can aid the recall of these terms.

Some aids to spelling have been developed. Franklin Spellmasters are electronic gadgets similar to a personal organiser. The student can spell a word and it will be checked phonetically and, if spelt incorrectly, an alternative spelling is suggested. There are a variety of these aids available, some with a thesaurus and/or a dictionary. Computers have spell-check programmes and help the student reduce spelling errors.

ESSAY-WRITING

Essay writing can pose particular problems for the student with dyslexia. It is a complex task and the student may have difficulty in some or all of the following: understanding the title, organising ideas and thoughts, finding the words to express these thoughts, spelling the words and then punctuation and handwriting. The student can cope better if he takes each of these in turn.

The first thing is to read the title of the essay and make sure that it is understood. Pay attention to the key words in the title. There are certain key words that occur constantly in questions and it is surprising how many students do not know their exact meaning. See Fig. 5.1 for terminology used in questions.

ANALYSE	Break into its component parts, discuss and show interrelations.
ARGUE	Make a case, using appropriate evidence, either for or against the issue.
ASSESS	Consider the value or importance of something, showing positive and negative points and give your point of view.
COMPARE	Identify features that two or more things have in common.
CONTRAST	Identify differences between two or more things.
CRITICISE	Judge the value or truth of a topic, showing your reasons.
DEFINE	Explain something in sufficient detail for it to be distinguishable from similar things.
DESCRIBE	Outline the main aspects of an idea, or show how a thing would appear to the five senses: taste, sight, touch, smell, sound. The five questions (how, why, who, where and when), will provide an mechanism to describe some events.
ENUMERATE	List or number points, possibly using a sentence to describe each.

EVALUATE	Judge the value or importance of something, showing positive and negative aspects.
EXPLAIN	Show how things work, or the sequence in their development. Describing could be part of this.
IDENTIFY	Show clearly the key features of a topic.
ILLUSTRATE	Similar to explain but should be accompanied by relevant drawings, diagrams, etc.
PROVE	Show the truth of a proposition, by presenting evidence to support your argument.
SUMMARISE	Reduce the text down to main points.
TRACE	Show the sequence of events or the interrelationships between topics.

Fig 5.1 *Terminology Used In Questions*
This list is a guide to the customary meaning of these words.

The next stage is to plan the essay. In a narrative type essay which may be given in Junior Cycle, the questions the student should ask himself are Who? Where? When? What? How? Why? and what was the result? This will help him structure his essay in a coherent manner.

Some essays are descriptive. A device to help the student include more description in what he writes, is to think of the five senses and write about the effect of the particular scene on each of the senses. An essay based on a description of a stormy day at sea could use this device as follows:

- ◆ Sight: what the clouds and sea look like, size of waves, the white foam, spray,
- ◆ Hearing: howl of the wind, crash of waves, seagulls crying,
- ◆ Smell: the odours of the sea spray,
- ◆ Feel: the cold touch of the wind, wetness of the rain and spray, the feeling of being blown along,
- ◆ Taste: the salty taste in the mouth.

In essays where he has to discuss or give opinions, he should take a sheet of paper and brainstorm the topic by writing down all the points that come into his head in any order. Then he should group linked ideas. This will help him develop the main outline of the essay, showing ideas he wants to include. It will also help to organise the format of the essay. Once this is done, it is easier to see the structure of the essay and the sequence of ideas. Parents may be able to help here by checking to see that the essay is in logical order and is related to the title of the essay. This will help with paragraphing. Each paragraph should deal with a separate point. The plan should have a clear introduction, development of the topic and a conclusion.

Having the master plan ready reduces the number of tasks the student now faces. The thinking and structuring has been done, he must find the words to express his ideas. Thinking about what he wants to say and expressing himself aloud may help him find the English he needs. A thesaurus is invaluable in finding the exact word.

Spelling is the next hurdle. It is difficult to suggest a way of handling this. Should the student look up spellings of which he is unsure and interrupt the flow of writing or should spelling be checked at the end and then be corrected? The answer to this depends on what works best for each student. Many students feel that if they stop to think about a spelling it can halt the creative flow. It is important to continue to write and get the ideas down. Mistakes in punctuation can be picked up if the essay is read out aloud on completion.

It is important that handwriting is legible, particularly if the student has to write in examinations and does not have access to computers. If the writing cannot be read, marks will be lost, so it is important to ensure legibility. Perhaps rewriting an essay after the thinking, spelling and punctuation have been completed will produce a more legible end-product. It is, however, very time-consuming and frustrating. Of course use of a word processor helps with spelling, grammar, presentation and editing.

WRITTEN EXPRESSION

The ability to express points is a key skill not only in English but also in other subjects. The Junior Certificate exam format suits students with dyslexia because in many of the subjects there are a series of brief questions in which they are asked to write short answers to demonstrate they know the facts. Handwriting, spelling and composition are less important in this type of answering. There is an enormous jump in the standard of answers needed at Leaving Certificate level. In many subjects at this level the student must be able to construct a longer essay-type answer and show what he knows. This can pose a challenge to the student who may find longer written answers involving organisation of information difficult.

The work of students with dyslexia when answering such essay type questions is often criticised for being too short. Use of guidelines or a prepared structure can help the student write more. Here are some examples.

◆ Frequently in English a student may be asked to discuss the traits of a character in a play such as Romeo in the play Romeo and Juliet. The student may write an answer such as 'He is romantic, brave, impatient and a good friend'. The student may believe he has answered the question, but in reality, instead of one line of an answer, the teacher expects a page at least and so marks are lost. However, if the student knows he must think up four different characteristics of Romeo and for each one, to describe two incidences in the play where Romeo showed this trait, his answer will be much longer and more comprehensive. By the time he has included an introduction and conclusion, his answer is much closer to the teacher's expectation.

◆ Another example is from History. The student may be asked to write about the life of a person in an ancient civilisation or a monk in medieval times. A list of items, which might apply to such a question, will prompt him to write more. Such a list could include: daily routine, transport, food, clothes, housing, power, crafts, burial, education and religion.

READING

Reading is a key skill at second-level. Most students with dyslexia have some reading skills but they need to pick up on speed and stamina. Such skills help them to access the information in textbooks across the curriculum. They often do not like reading. It can be so laborious that the story can get lost in trying to decipher the text. Yet if their reading is to develop, they must practise. It can be difficult to get books to suit the student. Books with a suitable reading level may have a very babyish content. Again the library service has books that may help. Some libraries have adult literacy schemes and have books with adult content, which have been abridged and the vocabulary simplified. These books can be graded for various reading levels. A routine of doing twenty minutes reading daily even throughout the summer can help develop and maintain reading skills.

When reading texts or suggested background reading, the student should read actively. This means he begins by being clear about the purpose of the reading, - what exactly does he want to find out? He should read with a pen in his hand, so he can take note of major points. Making notes will also help with his concentration. The student should check new words in a dictionary or thesaurus.

REVISION

Revision is an important element of work done at home. Written homework, learning homework and revision are the three ways which will help the student achieve. All are necessary. Written and learning homework will be given by the teacher. Both written work and learning by heart will ensure work done in class is understood and consolidate the material covered. However if the student does not revise, he will forget the content relatively quickly. Regular revision ensures that it is remembered. Part of the student's study timetable should include revision plans. A plan should be made out showing the subjects to be revised after homework each night. An example is given below for a Junior Certificate student.

MONDAY	TUESDAY	WEDNESDAY	THURSDAY	FRIDAY
History	Science	Maths	History	Business Studies
English	Irish	French	Science	Geography
Geography	Maths	Business Studies	English	Irish & French

The student in first year should plan to do two hours work a night. If homework takes an hour the rest of the time would be divided between the subjects for revision. If the student has a lot of homework one night, then the revision could be included in another night's work or the weekend. Adapt it to the student's personal schedule. If he has a scouts' meeting or a sports session one night, leave that night free of revision.

Setting goals is important in revision too. The student should make out a clear target to be learnt in the revision. The important aspect of revision is not the amount of time but the goals that have been met. A student can waste two hours sitting looking over his books and know very little at the end of the session. An example of such targeted revision could read as follows:

- ◆ In Maths, revision of ten theorems and do twenty examples from the textbook based on them.
- ◆ In Geography, revision of rock types, how to recognise them, where they occur, and what are their uses.
- ◆ In History, revision of how the monks lived in a medieval monastery, under the headings of work, food, manuscripts and clothes.

Coming closer to exams, revision becomes even more important. About six weeks before the exam, check that the student has the list of topics on which the examination will be based. This could be done on a single sheet of paper with a column for each subject. He may need help from teachers to do this as the student with dyslexia can have difficulty in quantifying and organising the work to be done. He then plans to cover a sixth of each subject list per week until the exams start. As he revises a topic he marks it off the list, so that he can see his progress on the chart.

This can also help reduce the anxiety before an exam. The student feels he is in control and he will have completely covered the course before the exam. This feeling of control helps minimise stress and anxiety. Stress is unfortunately part of the educational system. However, for students with dyslexia, stress and time pressures can make their particular problems worse and their thoughts can jump about and lack order. A clear revision plan, with clear goals, helps in keeping stress levels under control. Other well-known stress management techniques such as healthy eating and regular exercise also help.

PROJECT WORK

Projects can cause problems for students with dyslexia. These can include: difficulty in sourcing materials, in reading widely to pick out relevant points, in organising the structure of the project and in its presentation. Parents can provide vital assistance in all these tasks. It can give the student a sense of achievement to undertake a project and bring it to completion. When the student is given the project outline, help him work out a time frame for the various parts of it and set a completion date. He is learning valuable skills in organising projects and work as he comes to terms with his time goals. Selecting and narrowing the reading he has to do can help him as well. Computer skills are very valuable in project work as it helps in the organisation, presentation, layout and spelling of the final result. It means that these students can produce a project that looks professional.

CONTACT WITH THE SCHOOL

Parents should ensure the school has a full profile of the student by sending in copies of psychological assessments. It is helpful if they make suggestions based on their experience on what might work best with the student and that these are as specific as possible. Examples of such recommendations could be that notes be photocopied, that the student use revision handbooks or that the student be allowed to produce homework done on a computer. It can strengthen the parents' requests if suggestions such as these are backed by the psychological assessment.

However even if parents have given the psychological assessment to the school principal, they should not assume that all teachers will be informed of its contents. Schools are large complex organisations and all relevant members of staff may not be informed. The student will have up to ten teachers each year. I suggest making out a sheet explaining the difficulties of the student and any recommendations on which teaching methods might work best for the student. Parents could arrange to see the teachers individually and give them this sheet. Parents could also send it to the substitute teacher if a teacher is going to be absent for a period of time. If reading aloud in class is a major difficulty for the student, teachers need to know this on the first day the student is in the class so that they will delay asking him to read aloud. On that first day, the students coming from many different feeder schools are judging each other. If the student cannot read aloud, it will be part of this evaluation. However after a few weeks, when the student has found his place in the class, the fact that he cannot read with ease, will not have the same impact with his peers.

Parents should check if the student would benefit from an exemption from Irish and ask the school if the student qualifies under the regulations set out by the Department of Education and Science. They should contact the school to discuss whether to apply for reasonable accommodation in the state examinations for their child. If the application for reasonable arrangements is turned down, there is an appeals procedure.

OTHER ACTIVITIES

I have mentioned in the first chapter that self-esteem may be low in the student with dyslexia. At second-level he may find subjects that he has an aptitude for and will enjoy. However many subjects still have a high verbal content and the student may be struggling and still experiencing a sense of failure. Self-esteem gives the student the confidence to try out new experiences and to feel he can manage life. A belief in one's self is the key to the transition to an independent adult life. It can be fostered by the student being involved in extra-curricular activities and becoming competent in them. Involvement in sport, obtaining awards such as scouting badges, involvement in community activity such as visiting old people; developing skills such as photography or life-saving; being competent on a musical instrument; getting work experience; these are all activities which can foster self-confidence. Parents can play a role in getting students involved, particularly at an early age. As the student goes through the teenage years, the influence of parents diminishes. It should be remembered that all of these activities contribute to a Curriculum Vitae.

KEEPING GOING

Throughout this chapter I have mentioned ways parents can help the student. These all take time and effort over a long period of time. It can be very fatiguing. It is easy to start the year with good resolutions but to keep going consistently through the long months can be tough. It must be remembered that students have to work so hard in comparison to their peers simply to keep up with the class. They often have extra classes. A piece of learning might take them twice as long to do as other students. Writing an essay can be a strenuous exercise for them, whereas for another student it can be a pleasure. They can be tired and frustrated at times. And for all their hard work, they might not get the satisfaction of good grades. Parents also can feel the strain of providing consistent support. Sometimes, as a result, homework can become a flashpoint for irritation. This should be avoided. Such confrontations can undo a lot of good work done on self-esteem.

Parents must realise that they can make a contribution to the student's learning and progress that is irreplaceable. No one else can be there everyday on a one-to-one basis. However it is important for parents to realise they are only human and can only do so much. They should pick out the key three or four ways to help that they think most relevant and concentrate on those. I had to learn to do this over the years. My key points were note-taking and goal-setting. There are other suggestions in this chapter which would have benefited the boys but neither they nor I had the energy to pursue them.

The most important contribution parents can make is the development of a loving, secure relationship where the student is prized for himself and not his results and is given a feeling of support and parental backing.

Giving parental support is not a static process. At the beginning parents may be very involved in goal setting, checking homework, setting out revision plans, helping with projects but the intention should be that the student himself would develop these skills and would learn to apply these skills independently. How quickly this happens depends on many variables, such as the student's own abilities, his maturity and his relationship with his parents. It is a process that develops over a number of years. It is important to see the parents' help as a part of this process which will end up with the student taking responsibility and developing his own skills. If such gradual hand-over from parent to student does not take place, the help is a crutch and the student will become dependent on it. This may prevent the student progressing to independent adulthood.

Computers and Information Technology

6

Computers and information technology are of enormous help for all students but, in particular, provide essential and significant help to students with dyslexia. Such help is invaluable and this generation are very fortunate in having information and communications technology available to them. It is a form of liberation that can help them cope with the some of the effects of dyslexia. However the basic skills of spelling and reading still need to be in place to use the technology effectively.

Computers can help in the following ways:

◆ Help with student motivation. Computers can be fun to use.
◆ Programmes can be adapted to proceed at the student's own pace. There can also be immediate feedback, rather than waiting for the teacher's corrections.
◆ Assistive technology where the computer may help the student carry out tasks that they find difficult such as spelling or handwriting.
◆ Programmes which help diagnose dyslexic characteristics such as CoPS.
◆ Word processors which allow the student to present work clearly and legibly. This can help achievement and self esteem. It can also help the student do work faster.
◆ Programmes to help the student gain literacy and numeracy skills. Students with dyslexia benefit from multi-sensory teaching and repetition, both of which computers provide.
◆ Programmes to help develop study skills or organisation skills.

- Spell checks, grammar checks.
- Speech recognition software so the student can dictate to the computer and obtain a typed copy.
- Programmes which read text aloud to the student.
- Programmes based on the school curriculum which provide multi-sensory teaching of school subjects.

With so many programmes and products available, it is easy to become confused with the choice. Computer software is often expensive and comes packaged, so it is difficult to find out prior to purchase if a product is suitable. When buying a book in a bookshop, it is easy to flick the pages in order to scan the content and see if it is relevant. Looking at a software package is not as easy. It is difficult to see what it contains or if it is relevant for a particular student from the packaged product in the computer store. Ways of obtaining practical experience of the software include demonstrations of software at conferences or exhibitions, demonstration disks which can be available from suppliers or to be downloaded from the Internet or the student might be using a particular software package in school or in a DAI workshop and find it of benefit.

The technology is changing very rapidly and so information such as that contained in this chapter may go out-of-date very quickly. The web sites listed at the end of this chapter will provide a means of obtaining current information.

KEYBOARDING SKILLS

At the present time, the main method of inputting information into the computer is keyboarding. To be able to use a word processor effectively, touch typing skills or at least keyboard familiarity using eight fingers are needed. It takes the investment of time and effort to persevere to learn to touch-type, but is well worth the effort particularly for the student with dyslexia who will benefit so much from using word processors. It is very difficult for a person who uses the two finger approach and looks at the keys to change over to touch-typing so developing these skills as early as possible is recommended. Some students are well motivated and can learn by themselves. Others may need the discipline that comes from a course of structured learning with a teacher. Like all skills, the skill needs to be practised if it is to develop and be maintained.

The reasonable accommodations allowed in State Examinations include the use of a word processor for a small number of students. If the school is to assess whether a student would benefit from using a word processor in exams, the student needs to be proficient in its use. This means for a Junior Certificate student, that good keyboarding skills would be in place by 2nd year. The student should also be able to produce homework and projects using a word processor.

The BDA on their website have an information sheet on keyboard skills and touch-typing. It includes the criteria for choosing a touch-typing package for students with dyslexia and the names of recommended packages. One of the key recommendations is that the package should not use any 'near-words' e.g. 'hed', 'kik' as these could confuse the student with dyslexia who is trying to learn to spell correctly.

DIAGNOSTIC AND ASSESSMENT PROGRAMMES

In 1996 the Computer Resource Centre at the University of Hull developed a diagnostic screening system called CoPS (Cognitive Profiling System (CoPS)) to be used in the four to six age group. It measured a child's reaction to various challenges on the computer screen. This has been developed into four programmes for different ages

- ◆ LucidCoPS for children between four and eight.
- ◆ LASS Secondary for individuals between eleven and fifteen.
- ◆ LASS Junior for individuals between eight and eleven.
- ◆ CoPSbaseline for children between four years and five years and six months.

All four use standardised norms researched in the UK.

LASS Secondary is the appropriate level for second-level schools in Ireland. It is self administered by students as a series of challenging and entertaining assessments in the form of games that measure literacy, reasoning and cognitive skills, including memory and phonics. Interpretation of LASS Secondary is straightforward – use of a standardised graphical profile makes it easy to spot students who are under-performing generally or in relation to their intellectual potential. Any difficulties of a dyslexic nature – i.e. caused by underlying cognitive problems in phonology and/or memory – can be swiftly identified. Detailed results can be readily accessed for analysis. LASS Secondary can also be used on a regular basis (e.g. every term) to monitor progress in reading and spelling, and to check development of phonic skills.

LASS Secondary has eight modules that can be used individually or in combination. It incorporates adaptive testing, so that the computer automatically adjusts the difficulty of the items to suit the ability level of each student. This means the assessment is faster, more efficient and prevents the students becoming bored by items which are too easy, or frustrated by tasks which are too difficult.

The LASS Secondary Assessment Modules are:

- Visual memory
- Auditory verbal memory
- Phonic skills
- Phonological skills
- Single word reading
- Sentence reading
- Spelling
- Reasoning.

These enable teachers to:

- Assess the student's attainments in reading and spelling.
- Measure discrepancies between actual and expected literacy attainment.
- Identify underlying problems in memory or phonological skills.
- Diagnose dyslexic type difficulties which will help if recommending an assessment.
- Obtain a reasonable estimate of the student's intelligence.
- Monitor development in reading and spelling on a regular basis.
- Measure progress in memory, phonological and phonic skills.

This book focuses in particular on the student at second-level. LASS Secondary is an invaluable programme for a second-level school.

International figures suggest an incidence rate of dyslexia is between 4% and 10% of the population. The figures in Ireland are much lower. In my opinion and experience this is due to the fact that there are students with dyslexia at present in the Irish educational system who have not been diagnosed. LASS Secondary provides help in identifying students at risk for whom a psychological assessment should be recommended.

All four programmes are available from Edtech Software Ltd., Murrisk, Westport, Co. Mayo.

ASSISTIVE TECHNOLOGY

Assistive Technology provides the student with help in doing tasks they find difficult. In the case of dyslexia, computer technology provides very real help for the student.

The main forms of assistive technology are:

◆ Word processors with spelling and grammar checks. These enable the student to provide written material of good quality. This is particularly useful if handwriting is poor and takes a lot of effort. It can be faster and easier than writing by hand provided the student has good keyboard skills. It is also good for self-esteem to see one's work look well. Editing and rearranging text is easy, so students do not have to rewrite laboriously to produce a final copy. This facility also helps students who have sequencing difficulties as it is easy to edit the text so as to rearrange the sequence of points. Mistakes are easy to correct as spelling and grammar checks are provided. Because the word processor minimises spelling and handwriting difficulties, students are free to concentrate on ideas and the way they want to express them. It encourages them to be more adventurous and creative. It helps the student organise work as it can be saved and filed on the computer. A small number of students each year are given use of a word processor as a reasonable accommodation in State Examinations. **Alphasmart 3000** is a machine that does word processing only. It can hold 64 pages of material in eight separate files in its memory that can be downloaded to a printer or to a computer for filing. It has a small screen displaying four lines at a time. It is exceptionally robust. The price is approximately 400.

- Speech Recognition Software (SRS). This allows the student dictate to the computer which produces a typed copy on the screen. More and more of these systems are coming on the market. Some older systems require that the person speak each word distinctly with a pause between each word. Others allow the person to speak naturally as in conversation. This is easier and faster to do, but needs a powerful computer. The programmes need to learn the voice of the person so it takes time to train a system to an individual's voice. The user also needs training in being consistent in giving commands and punctuation instructions. Developing accuracy is important for students with dyslexia, as they may have more difficulty identifying mistakes made on the screen and correcting them. Speech feedback is useful, where the computer reads back what it has written. A program such as textHELP will help in reading over the text, and identifying grammar and spelling mistakes. These systems need a powerful computer, a dedicated sound card and a good microphone. The microphone must be properly adjusted. Many of the difficulties experienced with speech recognition systems are caused by the microphone. **Dragon Naturally Speaking** is one such programme. Information sheets on speech recognition systems are available from BECTA, BDA and IANSYST.

- Programmes that scan text and read it aloud. **Kurzweil 3000 Version 4** is such a programme. It displays on-screen scanned printed material and reads this aloud. It can be used on texts suitable for young children all the way to college students. It is easy to see how such a system can benefit the student who is learning to read, but it is also of huge benefit to the second and third-level student who has to read complicated text a number of times to extract the main points. By hearing as well as reading the text, this task can become much easier. The programme will also display and read aloud Internet documents. It is possible to scan coloured documents although there is a cheaper version of the Kurzweil that only uses black and white. Text sections can be highlighted in different colours and users can note or extract text to produce a study outline. Users are able to read along, take notes and highlight relevant text on-screen. Language tools such as a dictionary, thesaurus and phonetic spelling capability provide additional support. It can scan in 40 languages and provide speech in languages such as German, French, Italian, Spanish, Dutch, English and Russian. Text is read aloud by a human speaking voice from 'Realspeak' which provides the user with much improved synthetic speech, to which it is easier to listen to. The student can add notes to the text, either written or by voice. The programme allows a student include voice notes of up to two minutes in duration at a time. Such a facility would allow the student answer questions on comprehension texts or short questions on Junior Certificate papers.

◆ **TextHELP.** This allows text to be read back and spoken as it is typed. Words can be highlighted as they are typed. There is a phonic spell checker which can speak the words aloud. There is a context based word prediction facility. As the user types the first letter of a word, suggestions are made in the word prediction list. This reduces the number of keystrokes used helping with speed and sentence construction.

◆ Franklin Electronic Publishers provide a range of digital books in a system using inbuilt memory and interchangeable ROM cards which can be accessed from a computer the size of a calculator. This contains built-in reference works such as a dictionary, thesaurus, and multilingual translators. Most of the dictionaries have a 'common Confusable' feature where a person with a spelling difficulty can guess how a word is spelt and the Dictionary comes up with a list of words that it might be, with definitions so that it is possible to confirm which one is correct. Franklin also supply a range of spelling correctors and thesauri which include phonic spelling correction. The Language Master speaks each letter, word and definition. It contains 130,000 words, 300,000 definitions, and 500,000 thesaurus entries. It also includes word games.

- **Quickionary** Reading Pen. This hand-held reading pen can scan a word or line from any printed text, display the words in large letters, read the word(s) aloud, and define the word. It is possible to use a microphone for private listening.
- **QuickLink** Pen is a 'Digital highlighter' for scanning information when away from the computer. It scans and stores the information and then downloads it to the PC. It is very useful for taking notes and quotes.
- Personal organisers such as the Psion Series. These are pocket sized and can include a diary, spreadsheet, database, word processing facility, calculator, alarm, E-mail facility etc. Some students with dyslexia can tend to be disorganised. Structuring their life with the use of such an organiser, helps in recall of important facts and deadlines.
- *Textease* is a talking word processing package, with many of the facilities of Desktop publishing. The speech options allow the user to listen to letters, words, sentences or all the text. In the Multimedia Version, video, animations and sound files can be added to pages.

PROGRAMMES TO SUPPORT LEARNING

- **Wordshark 2L** combines the excitement of computer games with learning to spell and read. It offers 26 different games that use sound, graphics and text to teach and reinforce word recognition and spelling. It is featured on the BDA list of useful software.
- **Starspell** helps develop spelling skills from the young child to the teenagers. It uses the Look-Cover-Write-Check strategy. Every word is spoken and many have pictures. It is possible to create personal lists of words. It is featured on the BDA list of useful software.
- **Numbershark** is a programme to help anyone improve basic numeracy. It uses a wide range of computer games to develop numeracy skills over a wide range of difficulty. It offers 30 totally different games covering addition, subtraction,

multiplication and division in ways which add meaning and understanding to these operations. It is suitable for ages 6 to adult, school and home. It is on the BDA list of useful software.

◆ **Curriculum based programmes.** Computer based programmes based on the curriculum of subjects provide multi-sensory teaching which is beneficial for the student with dyslexia. However at second-level in Ireland, there are not a lot of programmes based on the Irish school curriculum. Many of the programmes on sale are UK based. ROSK E Systems are developing programmes for the Irish curriculum and have at present programmes for Irish, French and German at Junior Certificate and Leaving Certificate level. Junior Certificate Maths at Ordinary level and Higher level are also available. Future plans include programmes for Biology and Geography at Leaving Certificate level.

◆ **Inspiration.** People with dyslexia often prefer to think in pictures rather than in words. They like to use Idea Mapping – to build a visual map of ideas using pictures, colours, shapes and relationships. They use the technique for note taking , for remembering things and for organising ideas for written work. Inspiration allows the student build pictures on screen and then convert the image to a linear outline. It is possible to use textHELP to read and work with the outline. The outline can be copied into the word processor and used as a basis for writing.

◆ **Wordswork** is a multi-sensory approach to teaching study skills. It was designed primarily for undergraduates with dyslexia, but is very relevant for students at second-level and for adults who want to improve their skills before going back to formal education. It uses graphics, voiceovers, colour and humour to develop a variety of language skills which students with dyslexia (and others) need to address. Topics covered include:
• Essay writing
• Exam revision
• Grammar

- Handwriting
- Memory
- Oral presentation
- Punctuation
- Reading
- Spelling
- Time Management

The benefits of assistive technology are clearly illustrated by a student with dyslexia who is doing a BA in Social Care in DIT. She spoke at an AHEAD conference in 1999. She described her experience of going to college in the following terms.

'Since I started college I have never been happier. I've gone from total frustration and upset to loving my life. I do find the workload difficult and still have a problem keeping up with notes during lectures, as I get stuck on a spelling. When trying to spell a word I often lose a full paragraph of notes, as the lecturer cannot wait for me. This is frustrating especially since lecturers don't give out notes. Life has become so much easier due to the support as well as the fact that I received as assistive technology the Kurzweil 3000 and Dragon Naturally Speaking. The Kutzweil 3000 reads the material I need aloud to me. This gives me independence as I don't have to rely on Mam and it saves me a lot of time. Reading a chapter for college used to take me a lot of time, as I needed to read through it for difficult words, then had to look up these words, write in their meanings and read it through again to get an idea of the text. Finally I had to read it to pick up the relevant information and take notes. Now instead of three to four hours, it takes me forty-five minutes to an hour as I can speedread with the Kurzweil, highlight the relevant parts, look up as many words as I need to, cut and edit to make out revision notes, all at the same time. The Dragon Naturally Speaking also saves me time as usually I spend so much time concentrating on my spelling that I lose my train of thought and cannot focus on the correct way to phrase my words. Now I dictate what I need to write, without worrying about spelling. The words appear on the screen, and after a few adjustments, it is ready to be printed. All this has helped me so much that for the first time in my life, I passed my exams for the last two years with all honours.

GRANTS FOR EQUIPMENT AT SECOND-LEVEL

Circular M11/95 from the Department of Education and Science outlines the grant scheme that allows for the purchase of equipment for students with a disability. It applies to students who have been diagnosed as having serious physical and/or communicative disabilities that make ordinary communication through speech and/or writing impossible. It is possible that students with dyslexia could be considered under the communicative disabilities element of the scheme. The approval of the Department is needed prior to purchase and the scope of the scheme is limited to the funds available. The equipment remains the property of the school but is provided for the designated student. A recent comprehensive and professional assessment of the nature and extent of the disability and the equipment most appropriate should accompany the application.

FURTHER INFORMATION AND CONTACTS

British Educational Communications and Technology Agency (BECTA) Web: www.becta.org.uk
Information sheets on
- Special Needs and ICT
- Dyslexia and ICT

British Dyslexia Association (BDA) Web: www.bda-dyslexia.org.uk
Information sheets on
- Which computer and what will it cost
- Keyboard skills and touch-typing
- Literacy Software
- Maths Software
- Your computer talking to you
- Talking to your computer (Speech Recognition Software)
- Study Support Software

Daly, T. *Enabling Technologies, Guidelines for the use of Assistive Technology in Education.* A book on Assistive Technology produced by the SOLAS project, based in Boherbue Comprehensive School, Co. Cork. Web: www.enabletech.ie

IANSYST Ltd.,
The White House, 72 Fen Road Cambridge, CB4 1UN, UK.
Phone 0044 1223 420101 Fax 0044 1223 426644
E-mail: sales@dyslexic.com Web:www.dyslexic.com.

NITEC National Centre for Technology in Education, Dublin City University, Dublin 9. Web: www.ncte.ie
> *Special Educational Needs and Information and Communications Technology* This booklet provides information on:
> - ICT in Irish education,
> - Department of Education and Science Grants,
> - How to apply for grants,
> - Use of the ICT in the classroom,
> - Names of Irish suppliers,
> - Web addresses of Special Needs discussion groups,
> - Useful websites.

Ott P. *How to detect and manage Dyslexia* Heinmann 1997
> This book contains a very informative chapter on computers.

IRISH SUPPLIERS OF SPECIAL NEEDS SOFTWARE
Andrews Award Systems
38 Pine Valley Park, Dublin 16
Phone: 01 4930011 Fax 01 4944252 Email: award@iol.ie
Overseas agent for Inclusive Technology, a specialist UK special needs ICT company and overseas agent for REM, an educational software company supplying special needs products. Programmes include textHELP, Wordbar, Smog readability, Penfriend, Quicktionary Reading Pen, Numbershark, Wordshark etc.

Ash Technologies
Unit 5B, M7 Business Park, Naas, Co. Kildare
Phone: 045 882212 Fax 045 882214 E-mail: infor@ashtech.ie Web:
www.ashtech.ie
Specialist supplier of ICT for people with visual impairments,
dyslexia and learning disability. Programmes include WYNN, a
reading programme

Carroll Educational Supplies
Unit 5 Western Industrial Estate, Naas Road, Dublin 12
Phone 01 4567279/80 Fax 01 4569998 Email: ces@indigo.ie
Distributor for SEMERC, a specialist UK special needs ICT company.
The catalogue includes textHELP, Penfriend, Number Shark, Word
Shark, Inspiration, Wordswork, Wordbar.

Diskovery Educational Software
Unit 10, The Stables Office Park, Portmarnock, Co. Dublin.
Phone 01 8038824 Fax 01 8038977 E-mail: info@diskovery.ie Web:
www.diskovery.ie
Specialist suppliers of educational software to Irish schools and
teachers. Supplier of TEXThelp, Inspiration, Wordshark, Textease,
Rosk E Systems programmes on Junior and Leaving Certificate
examinations etc.

Edtech Software Ltd.
Murrisk, Westport, Co. Mayo
Phone/Fax 1850923459 E-mail: info@edtech.ie
Supplier of Crick Software, Penfriend, textHELP, Wordshark,
Starspell, Lexia, Wordswork, Lass Secondary, and CoPS.

Jackson Technology
24 Kiltipper Ave, Aylesbury, Dublin 24
Phone 01 4518508/01 4624793 Fax 01 4518508 E-mail: djackson@iol.ie
Web: www.jacksontechnology.com
Specialist supplier of ICT for people with people with visual
impairments, dyslexia and learning disability. Supplier of Kutzweil
3000, Dragon Naturally Speaking and TextHELP

RBC Technologies,
Currahaly, Farran, Co. Cork.
Ph 021 7331866 Fax 021 7331862
Supplier of AlphaSmart 3000

ROSK E Systems
4 Ballyroan Road, Templogue, Dublin 16
Phone 01 4930790 Fax: 01 4930889 E-mail: info@rosk.ie Web:
www.rosk.ie
Developers of programmes based on Irish curriculum

Support Services at Second-Level

7

I have worked as a second-level teacher since 1982 and from my experience I believe that, at this level, there is a lack of knowledge about dyslexia and a lack of information on effective teaching strategies for students affected by dyslexia as well as other learning difficulties.

This comment does not refer to learning support teachers and resource teachers who have had specialised training and in-service courses on the topic of dyslexia. They have experience of dealing with the needs of students with diverse learning difficulties. Such teachers have extensive knowledge of how to teach literacy and numeracy skills to students including those affected by dyslexia. Many students with dyslexia have benefited enormously from the invaluable contribution made to their progress by such teaching. I am not a learning support teacher nor am I involved in teaching literacy and numeracy skills. For this reason, I have not included any discussion on the teaching of these skills in this book. I have focused on how school systems can provide support for the student with dyslexia and how subject teachers can help such students to learn.

The fact that many second-level subject teachers are not aware of the needs of these students is not surprising when one considers that there has been little or no input on dyslexia and other learning difficulties during the pre-service training courses in the past. Even now few teachers have done in-career training on the topic. The Task Force on Dyslexia made eight recommendations on teacher training, including the recommendation that pre-service courses at primary and post-primary levels should include input on Special Needs Education, both integrated within general courses and as an area of study in itself. Attention should also be given to ways in which the class and subject teachers can identify and meet the needs of students with learning difficulties arising from dyslexia.

At second-level there is a defined amount of knowledge to be conveyed during a class period and often the underlying assumption is that every child absorbs information from the teacher in the same way. Consider that at second-level a teacher may teach close to two hundred students in a week. Taking the conservative estimate of an incidence rate of 4% of dyslexia, this means that up to eight of those students could be affected. Dyslexia is not like a physical disability where the student can still learn through the normal classroom techniques. It affects the entire dynamic between pupil and teacher. Teaching is about communicating information. Dyslexia affects communication. The teacher may think he/she has effectively given information to the student but this may not be the case. If the teacher is not aware of the symptoms and effects of dyslexia, the student may be classified as careless, lazy or stubborn. An understanding of dyslexia by the teaching profession would minimise such problems.

There is very little published research about dyslexia in Irish second-level schools. In 1996 Robin and Simon entered a project on dyslexia in the Young Scientist Competition. Part of the project was concerned with the incidence of formally diagnosed dyslexia in the second-level school population. They also looked at the provision of support services for such students in second-level schools.

A questionnaire was sent to 10% of the second-level schools in the country (seventy-one in total). Fifty schools replied. This gave a response rate of 70%. A total of 24,407 students were covered in the fifty schools. The conclusions were:

◆ There was 0.84% incidence of students with dyslexia in the 24,407 students covered by the survey. This is very low in comparison with international statistics, which suggests a 4% to 10% incidence. Dr. B. Hornsby in her book *Overcoming Dyslexia* says, "It is safe to say that recognisable forms and degrees of dyslexia are present in 10% of children in the Western population. ....In only 2% can the dyslexia be considered severe". The British Dyslexia Association estimates that about 10% of children have some degree of dyslexia. The Minister of Education and Science Dr. Woods said on 15th August 2001, 'It was estimated in repeated surveys that 10% of people have some form of dyslexia and a further significant percentage have other reading, writing or learning difficulties'. This result of 0.84% seems to suggest that there were many students with undiagnosed dyslexia in the Irish school population.

◆ A small number of replies indicated that the schools were not aware of what dyslexia is or how it can affect students. One school said that as all their students went on as far as Leaving Certificate, it did not have any such students.

◆ The support services which psychologists recommend for students with dyslexia were not being provided in the majority of the schools surveyed.

Support Service	% of Schools making the Support Service available (% based on the 50 schools which replied)
Extra time in exams	24%
Questions read to them in exams	28%
Use of school computer in exams	2%
Use of school computer for classwork	4%
Use of school computer for homework	2%
Use of own computer in exams	0%
Use of own computer for classwork	10%
Use of own computer for homework	12%
Use of a tape recorder in exams	30%
Photocopies of teachers' notes	34%
Choosing texts which are available on tape	34%
Allocating a teacher with special responsibility for students with dyslexia	62%
Study skills training for students with dyslexia	26%
Screening procedures at entrance to second-level	54%

In 1999 the Dyslexia Association of Ireland published the results of a survey of its members. Among the findings of this survey were:

◆ Over two-thirds of parents surveyed believe that teachers were not aware of the needs of students with dyslexia.

◆ Only in one case in three was the problem of a student's dyslexia brought to the attention of the parents by the school.

◆ Only 26% of respondents said they were satisfied with the help their children received within the school.

◆ Almost a quarter of children were not diagnosed as having a specific learning difficulty until after the age of eleven.

These surveys point to inadequacies in the provision for students with dyslexia in the school system. Hopefully with the new legislation, increasing awareness of learning difficulties and increased spending on special needs education, the situation will change.

A key factor in improving the situation is the provision of teacher training, both in-service and pre-service. Second-level schools are entitled to one day's in-service training for the whole staff once a year. Using this day to give the whole staff information on dyslexia and other learning difficulties would be an immediate and effective way to provide such training.

Below are some ways in which the school administration, school structures and exam structures can help the student.

EXEMPTION FROM IRISH

Irish is a compulsory subject and all students in Ireland have to study it as far as Leaving Certificate. Rule 46 of the Rules and Programme for Secondary Schools allows some students an exemption from Irish. One of the grounds for such an exemption is that it is given to students who function intellectually at average or above-average level but have a specific learning difficulty of such a degree of severity that they fail to achieve expected levels of attainment in basic language skills in the mother tongue. The guideline is that the student is in the bottom 10% of achievement.

In most schools an alternative subject to Irish is rarely provided. This means the student has one less subject in state examinations and also has extra free time. Many students with an exemption end up at the back of the Irish classroom doing homework. If the school could provide something constructive to do in this time such as giving the student English reading, extra tuition or extra computer time, it would be a positive use of this free time.

PROVISION OF ADDITIONAL LEARNING SUPPORT/RESOURCE TEACHING

In the *Learning Support Guidelines,* published by the Department of Education and Science in 2000, the criteria for the provision of such support at primary level were clarified. The Guidelines set out that supplementary teaching be provided to students who have not yet achieved basic competence in English and Mathematics i.e. those performing below the 10th percentile on nationally standardised tests of literacy and numeracy. At second-level while there are no such published guidelines, most of the learning support would be directed at students with similar numeracy and literacy levels. This means that students with dyslexia, whose scores may be higher than this, may not benefit from learning support.

There has been a huge increase in the provision of resource teaching hours, both full-time and part-time at second-level schools since 2000. A major difficulty is the lack of trained resource teachers as there was no course available prior to 2000.

In 2000 a two-year programme of training was introduced by the College of Education, Rathmines, for existing teachers at second-level. The National Training Programme for Resource Teachers (second-level) leading to the Diploma in Special Educational Needs has a total of fifty places, twenty-five in each year. Applications forms are available from the College and the closing date for applications in 2002 was in May. Year 1 spans the academic year with the time divided between attendance at the course venue, completion of written assignments and teaching in the participant's own school. There are a total of six weeks spent in the college. Year 2 spans the academic year as in year 1. There are ten weeks of lectures and seminars at the course venue. There are three weekend seminars, a block release week for study and reading, and a week's placement in an educational or clinical setting.

In 2002 a Post Graduate Training Programme leading to a Higher Diploma in Special Educational Needs was introduced in St. Angela's College, Lough Gill, Sligo. The programme spans an academic year and there are twenty-five places. Participants attend lectures and workshops for ten weeks. Three weekend seminars will be arranged during the year. There will be one placement in a special educational or clinical setting and one week of reading/study leave.

Circular 08/02 outlined the role of the resource teacher and the classes of student entitled the provision of resource teaching hours at primary level. The post of resource teacher is an additional post allocated to assist a school or cluster of schools in providing an education that meets the needs of children assessed as having disabilities. The disabilities listed in the circular include:

- Physical disability
- Hearing or visual impairment
- Emotional disturbance and/or behavioural problems
- Severe emotional disturbance
- Borderline/mild general learning difficulty
- Severe/profound general learning difficulty
- Autism/autistic spectrum disorders
- **Specific learning difficulty**
- Specific speech and language disorder
- Multiple disabilities.

The circular states that to qualify under the heading Specific Learning Difficulty, students must have been assessed by a psychologist as

- Being of average intelligence or higher
- Having a degree of learning disability specific to the basic skills in reading , writing or mathematics which places them at or below the 2nd percentile on suitable standardised norm-referenced tests.

Children who do not meet these criteria, and who, in the opinion of the psychologist, have a specific learning difficulty are more properly the responsibility of the learning support teacher and/or class teacher.

There is no such circular available for second-level schools. However the criteria being used in allocating resource hours at second-level must be broadly similar because at present these are the types of students who are receiving extra resource teaching. The application for resource teaching hours by the schools is made in February. The school should therefore inform parents of incoming students that psychological reports should be sent into the school by the January prior to entry. This means that in the case of students for whom resource teaching is appropriate, the school can apply in time and have the additional resources in place by September of entry.

Applications are made by the Principal of the school and must include details of the pupil(s), details of disabilities, an assessment by the Principal of the quantity and type of additional resources required, and copies of existing reports. New Assessments may be required when a previous one is out-of-date. The area psychologist investigates the application, assessments are undertaken, if required, and recommendations in respect of the additional resources are made, following discussion with the Principal and relevant teachers.

These criteria leave a gap in the provision of additional help for many students with dyslexia. Such students, whose intelligence can range from below average through to superior, may not fall within the bottom 10th or 2nd percentile in literacy and numeracy. However they may still experience difficulties at school. In Chapter 2 the difficulties listed included spelling, handwriting, expression, notetaking, sequencing etc. As a result of these difficulties they are not achieving their full potential but they do not qualify for additional help in school. The DAI workshop classes and exam preparation classes provide an example of the targeted help that can be provided for such students. In my own school, St. David's, in the school year 2001/2002   there were fifty-three students with diagnosed difficulties ranging from dyslexia to Attention Deficit Disorder (ADD) and Asperger's. Approximately twenty-five students were receiving learning support or resource teaching. The other students were in middle or top stream classes and so had to cope for the most part with the effects of their difficulties by themselves or with additional support provided outside school.

A number of parents of students in private second-level schools raised with the Task Force difficulties they encountered in accessing support services for their children since the Department of Education and Science does not sanction the appointment of learning-support teachers in some recognised private second-level schools. The Task Force recommended that the Department sanction learning support posts on a needs basis in such schools.

SPECIAL ARRANGEMENTS/REASONABLE ACCOMMODATIONS IN STATE EXAMINATIONS

Up to the year 2000 the term 'special arrangements' described the provision of supports for students with disabilities or difficulties when taking state examinations. This term then changed to 'reasonable accommodations'.

The report of the Expert Advisory Group on special arrangements in state examinations was published in 2000. The Minister of Education and Science accepted the general set of principles outlined by the Advisory Group and as a result circular S11/2000 was issued. The revised arrangements which are relevant to students with dyslexia are:

◆ Extra time to be given for the exam. The Advisory Group recommended that the time element of an exam be less critical. As a result, an additional twenty minutes was given for each exam session in the subjects, Irish, English, History and Geography in the Leaving Certificate examination. All students taking the exam can avail of this time. Other than this provision, extra time is not granted to students with dyslexia.

◆ Applications for reasonable accommodations will now be considered for a student whose intellectual ability is below the average range, but who has a specific learning difficulty.

◆ Up to 2000 there was no indication on the actual certificate or on the statement of results that a student had availed of special arrangements. The circular S11/2000 introduced an explanatory note on the certificate and the statement of results in language subjects. The wording of this statement can vary depending on the reasonable accommodation and is given below. If the student does not participate in a section of the exam, he/she will be marked out of 100% for the rest of the exam.

◆ The following accommodations are available if appropriate to the needs of the student:

- Reading Assistance. A reader should only be granted where a candidate is unable to read the question paper. This means the candidate must have a severe reading difficulty and that in the absence of the assistance of a reader, the candidate would be unable to take the examination at all. The explanatory note will read *'all parts of the examination in this subject were examined except the reading element'*.

- Tape recorder or computer. The use of a tape recorder or computer is appropriate where it can be established that the candidate has good oral ability, good knowledge of the course content, a score well below average on a spelling test and more than 20% of the target words unrecognisable under test and on written samples. The explanatory note on the English result will read *'all parts of the examination in this subject were assessed except spelling and written punctuation elements'*. In the other language subjects it will read *'all parts of the examination in this subject were assessed except for the spelling and some grammatical elements'*.

- Exemption from the spelling and grammatical components in language subjects. This exemption is considered appropriate where it can be established that the candidate has good oral ability, good knowledge of the course content, a score well below average on a spelling test and that the target word is easily recognisable as the target word, although mis-spelt. The explanatory note is similar as for the tape recorder or computer.

◆ Prior to 1999 there had been the facility to obtain a special arrangement whereby an examiner was notified by letter of a student's difficulties. The format of this letter varied over the years. The following is an example of the wording: *'The examiners to whom the above named candidate's scripts will be assigned for correction will be informed of the school's concern regarding the readability of his/her work and will be instructed, if they have difficulty in reading the scripts, to send them to an examiner who is more experienced in marking work which is difficult to read because of mis-spellings, bad handwriting, poor grammar, etc. Every possible effort will be made to mark the candidate's work reliably in accordance with the marking scheme and to ensure that he/she is given full credit for all the work done.'* This meant it was brought to the attention of the examiner that the student had difficulties. Since 1999 examiners are given the instruction to refer to their advising examiner any material they have difficulty in accessing. This applies equally to all scripts and so the scripts of students with dyslexia are not flagged.

Applications for reasonable accommodation are made by the school. The school sends the application to the Department of Education and Science and includes a psychological report and samples of the student's work. If an application is turned down by the Department of Education and Science, there is an appeals procedure. The members of the group dealing with appeals is drawn from people outside the Department of Education and Science.

Approximately 120,000 students sit State examinations annually. The numbers granted reasonable accommodations in the past are:

	1996	1997	1998	1999	2000	2001
Letter to examiners	918	1164	1343	–	–	–
Tape	77	107	133	222	319	379
Reader	151	168	200	350	562	791
Word Processor	7	4	5	10	12	14
Waiver Spelling and Grammar	–	–	–	–	–	1232

It is important that there is an objective assessment by the school of which reasonable accommodations, if any, would be appropriate for a particular student. Sometimes parents may be looking for any possible help and yet such help might not be appropriate or helpful to the student. Ways to help determine what accommodations are appropriate can include:

- That teachers mark house exam scripts in language subjects twice, once including the marks for spelling and grammar, and then excluding these marks to see if there is a significant difference in overall marks obtained.
- Ask the student to prepare for a test on a particular topic. An exam on this material can be given in traditional format and then by using a tape, word processor or a reader. Again the purpose would be to look for a significant difference in marks obtained.

If the use of a word processor might be appropriate, a preliminary step is the development of excellent keyboarding skills early on at second-level. Otherwise it would not be possible to ascertain if the use of the word processor would be of benefit.

If a particular form of reasonable accommodation is considered appropriate, such accommodation should be given in the house exams in the school. Indeed it is essential that the mock exams prior to the state exam be taken using the accommodation granted. This is very demanding on school resources to provide such accommodations as it can mean that a teacher has to be freed to take such exam students on a one-to-one basis. It may be possible to use parental assistance to help out or to train transition year students to act as readers or supervisors of taping of the exams.

The student will also need training in the use of the accommodation granted. It can be stressful to take an exam aloud with an adult present. Repeated practice can reduce this stress. The student also needs to know the role of the supervisor and the help they can give. In reading aloud the supervisor can only read what is on the paper, but the student can request particular sections to be reread as frequently as needed. In taping answers, the student needs practice in giving the exact details, the number and section, of the question he is answering. Answers when taping may be too short, possibly because the student cannot check what he has already answered easily, whereas with a written answer, it is possible to quickly scan the answer above. Another reason for short answers might be because of embarrassment in the one-to-one situation with the supervisor. The school appoints for the supervisor for exams taken with a reader or taping, and it can be someone with whom the student is familiar. This can reduce the embarrassment. The student could also use some blank paper to help structure his answer by making a list of the points he is going to include before speaking to the tape.

In the case of the reasonable accommodations of reading assistance, use of a tape or word processor, the student is in an exam centre by himself. The fact that the student is separated from the rest of the student body during the exams is a very public statement. This is at a time of development in adolescence when many young people want to be part of the peer group and do not want to be considered different. As a result some students will opt not to use the accommodation even if granted. It is important to prepare the student when applying for the reasonable accommodation by showing the tangible benefits by way of higher grades and also to prepare him for the one-to-one format of the examination.

The introduction of the explanatory note on the certificate is a cause of concern to the Dyslexia Association and to parents. It is a permanent statement on the certificate of the student. For future employers, who may not be familiar with dyslexia and its effects, the wording of the different explanatory notes might imply the student cannot read, or spell or use grammar at all. This is more important to the student who opts for employment after second-level. There is no such explanatory note on the certificates, diplomas and degrees issued by third-level colleges, and employers in all probability will not ask to see the Junior or Leaving Certificates of applicants with such qualifications. The Task Force on Dyslexia recommended that the practice of appending explanatory notes on the certificates be referred to the Director of Equality and the National Disability Authority.

Many parents, worried about the explanatory note, would prefer not to apply for accommodations if the student can cope at all with the traditional format of the exam. Therefore when deciding whether to apply for the exemption from spelling and grammar elements of the exam, a key factor may be the amount of marks allocated for spelling and grammar. For example, if the allocated marks are 10% or less, a parent might consider the student could cope without the exemption and pass the exam based on their knowledge, whereas if the allocated marks were more than this percentage, it could lead to the student failing the exam. However if a student is applying to CAO, availing of this facility means the student could increase his points score as a change of grade, for example C_2 to C_1, results in an additional five points. For these reasons it is important for parents to know the marks allocated for spelling and grammar. The Chief Examiner in English has stated the marks allocated for spelling and grammar are as follows:

♦ At Junior Certificate, higher level, 15 marks out of 70 are allocated for spelling and grammar in the personal writing section and 7 out of 30 are allocated in the functional writing section. Elsewhere throughout the papers at higher, ordinary and foundation levels, answers are marked by impression, with spelling and grammar forming an integral part of that impression.

♦ For English at Leaving Certificate, higher and ordinary levels, 10% of the marks will be allocated to spelling and grammar in Papers 1 and 2.

Marking schemes in the other language subjects are available from the Department of Education and Science and are published on its website, www.education.ie. These include details on how the scripts of students availing of reasonable accommodation are to be marked.

The examiners of scripts in the state examinations are second-level teachers. Many teachers have not received formal training in how dyslexia presents in written work in either pre-service training or in-service. As a result they may not be aware of how bizarre the phonic spelling of some students with dyslexia can be. Examples from phonic spelling from students' work include the following:

♦ amjedidly for immediately,
♦ anctus for anxious,
♦ enchivative for initiative,
♦ aricaligest for archaeologist,
♦ barax for barracks.

The examiner might have to read such scripts out loud in order to perceive the word the student means. Correcting exam papers for students with dyslexia takes more time. Poor handwriting, bizarre spellings and poorly expressed facts can mean the teacher has to decipher the script to see if the student has the correct answers. One example of this is where a student lost six marks in a Science exam for saying that a bimetallic strip 'would bend' under heat. However he spelt 'bend' with six letters (bouend) and it was marked as an incorrect answer. If examiners do not have experience of dyslexic scripts, it is quite possible that they might consider answers spelt bizarrely as wrong and not refer the script to more experienced examiners. Such a concern is noted in the Report of the Task Force on Dyslexia. In the past the special arrangement whereby an examiner was informed of the individual student's difficulties meant the script of the student with dyslexia was flagged. This would alert them to such difficulties. Now such notification is not given and there is no flagging of these scripts. I believe that until the time all in the teaching profession have received training on the topic of dyslexia and other learning difficulties, examiners should receive training in how dyslexia presents in scripts. This could form part of the correcting conferences which are held in June when the examiners receive guidelines on the correction of scripts.

An example of the benefit of availing of appropriate reasonable accommodations can be seen from the following example from my own school. A student entered second-level who had been diagnosed as having dyslexia. He had attended St. Oliver Plunkett's Reading School in Monkstown. He had received remedial help and had good family support. He was co-operative and pleasant and always did his homework. At Christmas in 1st year he took History as one of his first exams. He got 8%. The teacher was unhappy to give him such a poor mark. He had worked hard during the term and had seemed to understand what was being taught. She was worried that his self-confidence would be badly affected by such a low mark. It was decided to read the exam paper to him and write down his answers. His marks went from 8% to 55%. He had got similarly poor marks in Geography and Science. His teachers gave the tests orally and his grades in Science went from 12% to 54%. In Geography his grades went from 11% to 44%. If the history teacher had not raised the issue of his grade, he would have failed his Christmas tests badly. As it was, he did quite well. Also the school would not have become aware of the huge discrepancy between his written and oral performances. Below are examples of his answers on the written test and his answers from the oral test.

Geography short questions	His written answer	His answer after the question was read to him and his answer written down
Magma is	volcanic metel	molten material inside the earth core
Three things that happen at the plate margins are	earthqua volceno	earthquakes volcanoes geysers
The three rock types are	ignus metamorphic	metamorphic igneous sedimentary
Three uses of limestone are		making churches making fireplaces
A slag heap is		dust from a coal mine
Weathering is		rain falls on rock, and wears the rock away
A permeable rock is a rock which		water gets through

His lack of ability to read accurately and quickly and to express his knowledge in written form were major impediments to his passing written exams, yet he had the knowledge if he was examined orally. In his case the school requested a reader and the facility to tape his answers in state examinations. He passed all his examinations at Junior Certificate and obtained four honours grades on higher papers.

COMMUNICATION AMONG THE STAFF

In another incident this student also provided an example of how important it is that all relevant school staff be informed of a student's difficulty. The student had a detention. The Year Head, who was supervising the detention, was not aware of his learning difficulties and handed out the usual assigned work. The student was not able to do it. At the end of the detention period he was given another detention because he had not done the required work. It was sorted out later but he was very upset, as was the Year Head when informed of the student's reasons for not completing the assignment.

A communications system should be set up which will routinely inform the staff of a particular student's difficulties. This could include giving a profile of the student's strengths and weaknesses, and suggestions about effective teaching and testing strategies. This information is highly confidential. If it is given in written form it is advisable to give the information on these students identifying each student by number only, and handing out a separate index.

REASONABLE ACCOMMODATION IN HOUSE AND MOCK EXAMINATIONS

If the student's difficulties are such that he is getting reasonable accommodation in state exams, it is only fair that such accommodation also be given in the house exams. This should be part of school policy on dyslexia. Teachers should be reminded of the student's difficulties prior to the exams and, if appropriate, arrangements made for him to take the exams by tape or on word processor, have the papers read to him or have an exemption from the spelling and grammar elements of the language subjects.

If sending mock papers outside the school for correction, a note should be attached to the paper explaining that the student is receiving reasonable accommodations in the state exams. An incident which illustrates the importance of such communication is the case of a student with dyslexia who sat a Junior Certificate higher level English mock paper. The paper was returned with the comment that the spelling was so disgraceful that higher level English was out of the question. This had a negative effect on the student's confidence when sitting the actual exam in the Junior Certificate.

PHOTOCOPYING NOTES AND USE OF REVISION BOOKS

All students can benefit greatly from good notes. It is more beneficial that a student summarise his textbooks himself as it helps him absorb the information. However it is likely that students with dyslexia will find it very difficult to summarise material in books and make their own notes. This can be due to poor or slow reading where they may have to reread a piece several times to see the points the writer is making, difficulties in summarising and organising material or difficulties in the presentation of legible and clearly laid-out notes. The essential task is to learn the information. Having to make their own notes from the text can place additional barriers in their way.

These students can therefore benefit hugely from getting precise and concise notes. The source of such notes could be teacher notes, or copies of the notes of other students. Good notes give them the means to learn. Some students with dyslexia have difficulty seeing and organising patterns. Good notes are an effective way for them to see the structure of what they are learning. The notes are a useful device in organising material and are helpful in formatting their own answers. Because the notes are structured, the student can use that structure when answering questions. Revision handbooks are of use if the student is not provided with photocopied notes. I recommend, in the case of students with dyslexia or other learning difficulties, they use them from the beginning of first year when they start the Junior Certificate courses and from the start of fifth year for the Leaving Certificate.

If teachers dictate their own notes to the class, it can be a problem for students with dyslexia. Some students have a difficulty in visualising the words being called. They have to think about the shape of the words and then they have lost the next point the teacher makes. If necessary, the teacher should arrange for photocopies of notes to be given to the student. These could be photocopies of the teacher's own notes or a photocopy of the notes of a student who takes well-organised, legible notes.

Here is an excerpt from an essay a sixteen year old girl wrote about her dyslexia.

'My head ached, letters churned in my mind. I wanted to scream. I glanced at my friend's masterpiece, every word spelt correctly and a page of beautiful writing, the work teachers love. Slowly I looked at my own copy, half finished sentences, words spelt incorrectly. I placed my hand over my work, embarrassed in case any one would see it. As the Junior Certificate approached and more notes were being called out, the more lost I became. Each time a word was spelt out to me, it became more jumbled. I got so frustrated. I wanted to give up. I would go out with my friends, when deep down I knew I should be studying. But there seemed little point. I would study and make notes, but I seemed to remember very little. I know that something was wrong, but did not know what. Finally it dawned on me. Maybe I had a learning problem. I could not explain but I had a funny feeling it was dyslexia. I did not know much about it. My parents were very supportive. I was diagnosed as having dyslexia. In a way I felt relieved to know I had dyslexia and that I was not thick. I felt angry and confused and wished I did not have it. What angered me most was finding out two weeks before my Junior Certificate, as I worried I would not be able to spell words in the exam.'

She was a student who had gone through primary school without being identified as having dyslexia. When she did her entrance test, her scores were in the average range. There were no perceived weaknesses on her profile of ability. The use of the Dyslexia Screening Test or LASS Secondary may have helped to identify her earlier, but they were not available at the time. During her first three years in the school she worked very hard but was always disappointed at her results. She felt it took her much longer than others to absorb written material. She had to reread articles many times to make sense of them. She was spending longer hours on homework than the school would recommend. Prior to her Junior Certificate, the frustration of trying to take notes overwhelmed her. She could not visualise what she was to write when the teacher called out notes. She had developed coping mechanisms such as copying from a friend or waiting for others to ask the teacher to repeat a phrase. If the teacher spelt something out, she virtually had to translate the spelling into what the word looked like. If the teacher, when spelling out a word, said 'double O', she would have to ask herself 'what does that look like?' She spoke to her parents saying that she thought she was dyslexic. Her assessment showed this to be the case. Because she had worked hard and had learnt to read at the expected ages, she had gone undiagnosed until this stage.

Have a look at the notes in Fig.7.1 and ask which notes could you learn from best.

(A)

Implications of the Companies Act 1980

1. If a company has engaged in reckless trading, a director may become a restricted director. He may not be able to take part in a company for five years and loses limited liability.
2. A director involved in fraud or dishonesty may be disqualified for a stipulated period.

(B)

implecations of the
1. companies act, 1980
1 if the company has begon
in recless trading, a director
may become a restricted
director he may not be
able to take part in company
for 5 year and loss limited
leability
2 a director involve in
fraud or disgonsty may
be disqualified for a
stipulated period.

(C)

emplications of the companies act 1980

1. If the company has begoy in recless
   trading, a director may become a
   restricted director he may not be able
   to take part in a company for 5 year
   and loes limited liability
2. A director involve in frude or disonesty
   may be disqualified for a stipputated period.

Fig. 7.1   *(A) shows typewritten Business Organisation Notes which were dictated.*
(B) shows the notes taken by a student with dyslexia
(C) shows the typed written version of the student's notes

A school policy that would allow the photocopying of notes is of benefit to students with dyslexia.

TAPES

Tapes of notes or texts can help some students with dyslexia to learn. This might be apparent in the psychological report where good auditory memory is commented on. The material is being presented to two senses, sight and hearing. Teachers could suggest to parents or to the student himself that notes be taped, in order to see if this is beneficial.

In some subjects, in particular English, videos and tapes of texts are commercially available. If reading is very laboured, the student can lose the thread of the story because it is such hard work to decipher the text. Listening to a tape of a novel while he reads it can mean he can become engrossed in the story. He does not have to look up difficult words as he hears them. He can get familiar with characters and plots. If the poems he has to learn are taped, it can help him to become familiar with them. Videos of Shakespearean plays make the play come alive and make it easier to write about. It does not replace reading the play which needs to be done for the student's own reading development and to make him familiar with the spelling of names, but it helps his knowledge of the text.

In Junior Certificate English, the teacher has great freedom to choose texts. It makes sense that if there is a student with dyslexia in the class that the teacher would choose textbooks that are available on tape.

If the student is not a reader, the teacher could encourage him to widen his knowledge of literature by using tapes. For some students reading does not become any easier. They may have good functional reading skills but reading will never become a pleasurable activity. Part of their coping mechanism is to look for alternative ways to get information and be up-to-date with current books. Tapes, radio and television can provide other routes to information.

SCREENING AND IDENTIFICATION OF PUPILS WITH DYSLEXIA

Up to 1996 there has been no screening test for dyslexia, either at primary school level or at second-level. Psychological assessment was suggested by teachers if the child failed to achieve in reading and writing by the age of eight or nine. So, while it is likely that severely affected students would be identified, borderline students who achieved reading could slip through the net. Dr. B. Hornsby in her book *Overcoming Dyslexia* calls these students 'hidden dyslexics' and suggests it is only when their earlier promise is not fulfilled in exams that teachers and parents begin to ask questions.

Since 1990, over fifty students have been diagnosed as having dyslexia or other learning difficulties in my own school. All had gone through primary school without being identified or sent for assessment. Two students were identified from the Differential Aptitude Testing done in third year. One of these students had a percentile score of seventy-five in abstract reasoning and two in verbal reasoning. One student, out of frustration, had raised the question herself because of her difficulties in taking notes. Other students were identified from the entrance assessment where an uneven pattern of ability might raise questions. LASS Secondary is now being used in the school to help identify students with difficulties. In all cases a full psychological assessment needs to be carried out in order to make a diagnosis.

I believe that there are many students going through the education system in Ireland who have not been diagnosed and who are frustrated and confused by the demands made upon them. With the development of NEPS and increased teacher training as recommended in the Task Force on Dyslexia, hopefully this will become a thing of the past.

New screening tests became available in 1996 (See Chapter 2). Particularly important are the tests for the younger age group. It is important that students with dyslexia are identified in their early years at primary level before they start to fail and their self-esteem suffers.

The DST (Dyslexia Screening Test) is now available to help screen students in the age-group 6 years and 6 months to 16 years and 5 months. It could be used if a teacher has any suspicion that a student may have dyslexia. A second screening instrument is LASS Secondary. This is a computer aided screening test available since 2000. Such screening instruments should be available in all schools.

It is important that teachers be aware of inconsistencies and behaviour that might indicate dyslexia. These could include:

◆ Bizarre spelling, e.g. emplocashuns for implications
◆ Phonetic spelling of common words, e.g. tennice for tennis
◆ Omission of the endings of words, e.g. essa for essay
◆ Confusion about the shape of letters such as b and d
◆ An uneven profile of ability, e.g. very good maths but very poor verbal skills
◆ A mismatch between verbal performance and written performance
◆ A difference between verbal and abstract reasoning. It may be noticeable on the AH2 or AH4 test or on the Differential Aptitude Tests (DATS)
◆ Confusion about left and right, or direction
◆ Transposition of parts of words or letters inside a word or in a sequence of numbers
◆ Frequent loss of place when copying from the board or reading from a page
◆ Confusion about simple sequences such as the months of the year

- A slow rate of work, yet good results if ample time is given
- Difficulty in recognising rhyme, such as star, far, jar
- Badly formed handwriting
- Difficulty in following a sequence of directions.

A combination of several of these indicators should lead teachers to question whether there is a specific learning difficulty present. The use of DST or LASS Secondary may help confirm suspicions. The teacher should then consult with the student's parents. It is only with a psychological assessment that a diagnosis of dyslexia can be made. The development of NEPS should help in accessing assessments. In schools where NEPS are not providing a service, a fund of £1.5 million was established to allow schools finance assessments from the private sector. When parents pay for the assessment, the cost can be claimed as an expense for income tax purposes.

STANDARDISED TESTS

Standardised tests are tests given under very strict conditions. The purpose of the test is to give a result which shows how a student achieved in relation to the population of students of the same age and sex. This is done by comparing the result to norms that have been researched. Such standardised tests include the Micra T tests, Drumcondra Tests, Differential Aptitude Tests (DATS), AH2 and AH4.

For some of these tests timing is critical. Students are not meant to finish the test in the time allocated. The score is derived from how far they get through the test in the time allotted. In other tests the time is not so important. The allotted time is so generous that the vast majority of students will have answered all the questions with plenty of time to spare.

It may be difficult to get an accurate result on such tests for the student with dyslexia for the following reasons:

- The student may be slower in processing information. Here is an example based on the DATS (Differential Aptitude Testing). There is a generous time allowance for completing all but one section of the DATS. The vast majority of students finish the questions well within the time allotted. A student with dyslexia in my own school did the Numerical Reasoning section. The student completed twenty-seven out of the forty questions consecutively and then ran out of time. All of his answers to that point were correct. It was obvious that with more time this student would have completed more questions and obtained a higher score. His result is different to the student who has completed the full forty questions within the allotted time and got thirteen incorrect. Yet both students would be given the same result.

◆ The student may be slower in reading the instructions or in deciphering the sequence of instructions. They may lack the vocabulary to be able to do the task required. This is critically important in Maths testing. Here is an example of a Maths question from a standardised test.

'John spends three times as much as Michael on Bus fares each week and Michael spends three times as much as Martin. If John spends 45p, how much does Martin spend?'

For some students with dyslexia such a question is more a test of their English skills than their Maths abilities. They may need time to work out the words mean and to interpret the sequence of instructions correctly. This makes their work much slower and sometimes they may not successfully decode what it is they are meant to do.

An example from another standardised test is as follows. It is a test of the student's ability to classify. They have to choose the odd one out from a series of words such as the following: *Butcher, vicar, grocer, baker.* The students are given forty such problems, and a limited amount of time in which to answer. No student is expected to complete the entire test. The score is based on how far they progress in the test. Lack of vocabulary and slowness in reading the words on the page can slow down their answering. It is the processing of information and their reading skills that affect their scores

It is important that parents, students, and teachers realise the limitations and unreliability of these tests for students with dyslexia and other learning difficulties. **They are not valid predictors of the student's ability**. However such students are likely to have a far more valid instrument of their ability in the psychological assessment.

At primary level, no critical decisions are made based on standardised tests. However the results could affect the child's self image. Despite being told not to, students do compare the results achieved. Therefore it is important that the child understands the results are not reliable. Also, if a teacher has not received training on the topic of learning difficulties, he/she also might form expectations of the child based on the results of standardised testing. This is why it is so important that the psychological assessment is brought into school and the student's profile with its strengths and weaknesses is discussed with the teacher.

Far more important is the fact that these tests may be used at Entrance Assessment at second-level. Crucial decisions may be based on the student's performance in this assessment such as class placement.

The Civil Service Commission allows students with dyslexia additional time when taking standardised testing for recruitment purposes.

EXTRA CURRICULAR ACTIVITIES

Most writers on dyslexia describe the effect it has on self-esteem and confidence. The student has experienced failure from a very early age in a key part of life, that of academic achievement. It is also a very public arena since all students in a classroom know the student who has difficulties in achieving. This failure in academic achievement can ripple through many aspects of life affecting relationships with peers, leading to a lack of confidence that may lead him into not trusting his abilities and being unwilling to try or join in new experiences. The lack of confidence may be worse if the dyslexia is not diagnosed until second-level.

Some students may find an escape mechanism from being thought 'stupid and thick' by avoiding school work and by confronting authority. It is more acceptable among the student's peers that poor grades are the result of being a 'tough' man rather than the result of a learning difficulty. Others have become expert in evading work. Since many teachers have not been trained to recognise and deal with dyslexia, these students can get away with these avoidance tactics. This highlights the need for teacher training.

As part of school policy, some brief description of dyslexia and how it affects students should be given perhaps in the pastoral care programme or the study skills programme. It makes it easier for the student to be open about difficulties when other students understand about dyslexia. He may also realise that other students can also be affected and that he is not alone.

Students with dyslexia are likely to experience failure to some extent in their academic studies. If self-esteem and confidence are to be developed it will be in other aspects of life. It is really important that these students get involved in activities where they can achieve and be part of the wider school community. Sometimes, because of their low self-esteem, they will be reluctant to join in extra-curricular activities and may need active encouragement from parents and school staff. Types of activities may include all types of sports, clubs, drama, voluntary work and projects. Part of the support service the school should offer is active intervention in encouraging these students to become involved in such activities.

SCHOOL STRUCTURES

Below are some pointers to what could be included as part of the support services for students with dyslexia.

- ◆ If the student has exceptionally weak reading and writing skills, is there an assessment to check if there is a significant difference in his exam performance if he takes an exam orally with a reader or with a taping facility? This would be to check if it would be appropriate to apply for such facilities in State exams.
- ◆ If reasonable accommodation is given for state examinations, is it available for house exams?
- ◆ If the student's verbal skills are so poor that he might have difficulty understanding the format of questions in the

entrance assessment, does the school make a reader or other assistance available to him? Whereas a reading test will give an accurate picture of his reading skills, a Maths test, where the student does not understand what he is being asked because of the language content or sequencing of the questions, does not measure his Maths ability.

- If there is streaming, does it take account of the student with dyslexia who may be very intelligent and articulate but who has some verbal difficulties?
- Is placing such a student in a lower stream class the best option?
- If places in a particular option are limited, would the school consider giving positive discrimination to such students when allocating places?
- If a student has excellent Maths but poor language skills, will the student have the option to do Higher Level Maths?
- If Irish is part of the entrance assessment and the student has an exemption from Irish, is there a mechanism to take this into account in the overall placement?
- If the student is exempt from Irish, is it possible to arrange for another subject or activity to be done during this free time?
- Is a third language obligatory in the option structure?
- Are students with learning difficulties given training in study skills?
- Is learning support available in first year? In later years? Is it available if the student is not in the weakest classes?
- Does the student have access to computers? Can extra computer time be made available so the student can develop good keyboard skills? If this cannot be done in school time, can it be arranged after school? Parents may be willing to pay for this.
- Has the staff received in-service training on dyslexia and other learning difficulties?
- Are staff reminded on a regular basis of the needs of these students?

HELP WITH THE TRANSITION TO SECOND-LEVEL

The transition to second-level may be daunting to the student with low self-esteem or with social difficulties. The second-level school is much larger both in size and in number of teachers and pupils. Possibly the student may not know any one else going to the school, so the first day is a major hurdle. A school in south Dublin has introduced a scheme to help these students cope. If parents tell the school that the student may be vulnerable, such students are invited to attend the school for an orientation day. This day is held the day before the term commences. They are introduced to the other students in the group, teachers, the layout of the school and the timetable. Part of the day includes games and quizzes on what they have learnt. On the following day, when the school opens for all incoming first years, these students have the edge. They can take the lead and show the other students around and can introduce teachers. They also know the other members of the group so they are not alone.

TASK FORCE ON DYSLEXIA

The Task Force on Dyslexia made recommendations about the provision of support services in second-level schools. These included:

♦ Under the Education Act 1998, Boards of Management are required to publish the school policy in relation to the participation of pupils with disabilities and the School Plan must state the measures that the school proposes to take to achieve equality of access and participation. The Task Force recommended the incorporation in the School Plan of whole-school procedures and strategies for identifying and addressing the needs of students with dyslexia.

♦ The key role of the Principal is recognised in creating a learning environment in which students with learning difficulties can develop. The Principal impacts at policy and practical level by promoting a 'dyslexia friendly' culture and ethos. The report of Task Force lists the steps the Principal can take to ensure this ethos.

♦ Parents should be involved in assessment of the child's learning difficulties, the development and implementation of individual learning programmes and in making decisions on continuation/discontinuation of services.

◆ The school should identify a named teacher with responsibility for the co-ordination of services for students with learning difficulties.

◆ Learning support teachers should play a pro-active part in advising and collaborating with subject teachers to co-ordinate class and supplementary teaching programmes for students.

◆ That, for each student with learning difficulties arising from dyslexia who is in receipt of learning support, the class teacher, learning support teacher and parents work jointly on the preparation of an individual learning programme designed to meet the student's needs and should review its implementation at least twice a year. The Report of the Task Force contains a list of the issues that should be addressed in such a programme.

◆ The interventions for students in the 12-18 age group should continue to focus on decoding, spelling/punctuation and writing, but should be extended to include self-regulated learning skills, note-taking, exam strategies, occupational exploration, access to subject knowledge, reasonable accommodation in exams, and in some cases strategies to encourage and assist the student stay in school.

◆ Where a student cannot study a subject, because of a specific learning difficulty arising from dyslexia (for example, Irish), schools should make appropriate alternative arrangements.

◆ A comprehensive record should be maintained for each student with dyslexia. It should include:
  • A summary of the student's progress in primary school.
  • Reports from subject teachers on the student's progress.
  • An individual educational plan.
  • Information on the status of the pupil in relation to exemptions from the study of Irish.
  • Information on reasonable accommodation provided for or sought for in-school and state examinations.

- Work samples provided by the student, under exam conditions.

If the recommendations from the Task Force Report are implemented, it will lead to huge improvement in the services for students with dyslexia in Ireland

How Subject Teachers Can Help

8

Some of the topics in the previous chapter would be relevant to the subject teacher such as note-taking and taping. However there are specific techniques that the subject teacher can use in the classroom that will help the student with dyslexia.

I appreciate how difficult some of these may be to implement for a busy class teacher. At second-level a teacher might easily deal with two hundred students in a single day and has classroom contact with a particular class for approximately three hours in a week. The Task Force on Dyslexia recommended that subject teachers 'provide differentiated instruction to students who have learning difficulties arising from dyslexia'. To tailor teaching techniques to meet individual needs takes time and time is at a premium. However some of these students will fail unless teachers are aware of their specific difficulties and try to find some teaching methods that will help them to achieve. Here are ideas that may help:

◆ The student may have great difficulty in deciphering script handwriting whether it is on the board, in notes or on exam papers. Teacher notes and test papers should be typed

◆ Break down a series of instructions into simple commands. Do not give an instruction which is a complicated sequence, e.g. 'After you have taken down your homework and before you leave the room, clean the desk'. Break it down to a series of simpler commands, 'Take down your homework', 'Clean your desk', 'Now you can leave' The student, who has difficulty with sequences or who has to decipher what is being said, gets confused unless instructions are kept simple.

◆ Some students with dyslexia have difficulty remembering sequences such as days of the week or months of the year and this can lead to conflict with adult demands. A student may have been given homework as follows: an essay for Monday, Maths for Tuesday, revision of a text in Geography for next Thursday, reading for a book report to be handed up in two weeks time. Teachers assume that the student will see time and sequence clearly in much the same way as they do. However, because of sequencing difficulties, he may confuse the instructions. He then gets into trouble with teachers for not having his work done. It is easy for adults to conclude that he is lazy or careless. To overcome this, ensure he uses a homework notebook properly with a system that will remind him of tasks.

◆ Give written notices of events. Most second-level students are more than capable of listening and taking home clear details. However it is very likely that students with learning difficulties will neglect to take home a key fact or they will give jumbled information.

◆ Some students will understand the sequence of steps in a Maths problem, a Science experiment or a book-keeping problem in class and appear to be competent but become confused over the sequence later. Whereas the average student might need to do an example four or five times to be sure of the sequence of steps, some students with learning difficulties may need to overlearn the sequence by doing more examples.

◆ Some students may not decode what it is they are being asked to do in a question. It is important that they are taught how questions are structured and what are the precise meanings of words used in questions. The student may misinterpret the small link words and yet these radically affect the meaning of a question.

◆ Check if the pupil is willing to read aloud. Some would prefer to do so and not be treated differently from the rest of the class. Others are very conscious that their reading skills are laboured and this anxiety can make their reading worse.

- When reading textbooks, introduce the content, so the student becomes tuned in to the gist of the material and keywords. This will help with comprehension. If it is a text with questions at the end of sections, get the student to read the questions before reading the text, so he knows what points are relevant.
- Be understanding when giving poetry or other sequences to be learnt off-by-heart. Some students find it exceptionally difficult to remember a sequence regardless of how much time they spend on it. Some do not register rhyme as a pattern. In learning poetry, if a verse has line endings such as: hood, good, wood, they are as likely to say forest for wood. They have understood the poem and know the ideas and content but they may not perceive the rhyming pattern.
- If the student has difficulty in structuring what he wants to say, arrange to give extra time so he can get his thoughts together. The same applies when asking a question. Remember some students have to decipher the question and then formulate their answer. This can put them under time pressure and adds to their anxieties and frustration in the class. They can spend a lot of time worrying about being asked questions. Under pressure they can resort to wild guesses. One technique which would help is if the teacher arranges with them (privately) that they will be asked questions only when the teacher is standing in a particular place. This will mean they can relax for the rest of the time and concentrate on what is being said. Another technique when asking them a question is for the teacher to ask the question, turn and write something on the board and then look for an answer. The student has had time to put his thoughts together.
- Some students have difficulty recalling the name of an object or person. A student could know all about Leonardo Da Vinci and yet have difficulty recalling his name. He might guess wildly or else pepper his description of Leonardo's work and times with 'you know your man'. Such students should overlearn the names of people and objects. One method of doing this is to use vocabulary notebooks which contain new

words and names in each subject. These can form the basis for revision just before an exam as it is these words that are most likely to have been forgotten.

◆ This next point is one that applies to me personally. I get totally mixed up about right and left. When being taught anything to do with motor skills, such as gym, using a computer mouse or learning to drive, I have to interpret and decipher what the instructor says. If the gym instructor says 'do this', and does a particular action, I have to break it down, analyse what he has done and work out how I have to move to copy it. Once I have learnt how to do an action, it becomes automatic. This illustrates the point that students who may not have academic difficulties may still be affected in other subjects with a motorskills element such as Physical Education, Home Economics, Technical Graphics, Science or Art. They have to interpret what they are being asked to do and then work out how to do it. It is as though they have to translate the instruction. This can make them appear slow and lacking in concentration.

◆ When correcting, be sparing in the use of red pen. Not all mistakes need to be marked. Take a particular category of error and correct it. There is a greater chance that the student will learn from this. A comment such 'improve your writing' will have little effect on the standard of writing. The student may not know how to improve his handwriting. Try to identify one fault which he can work on such as 'closing the loops in letters such as a, d, g'. Remember it will have taken the student longer than his classmates to produce this homework and it is disheartening if it is full of corrections. If the student has difficulty handing up nicely presented work, get him to use copies with fewer pages, so he has a fresh start more frequently. If the idea is right, give marks regardless of spelling, layout and presentation. Take time to check out bizarre spellings. Since self-esteem can be low, positive encouragement is needed, which is why it is so important that the student gets credit for work done. However for self-esteem to be fostered, the achievement of the pupil must be real. The student will be aware if praise is given for poor work and he could become cynical. This will mean he may not believe genuine praise given to worthwhile work.

◆ Order and structure may need to be taught to some students whereas most students at second-level have learnt how to lay out their work and organise their studies. Some ideas here would be to use Maths copies with squared paper to help keep figures in columns. Take the student aside and show him how you want a page laid out. Write out an example to which the student can refer.

◆ Since some students with dyslexia have a poor grip of the pen, which causes muscle strain, pens with padded tops can be helpful.

◆ Give him a structure for attempting longer written answers. Show him the question, breaking it down into its constituent parts. Too often his answers will be too short because he does not develop a structure. He feels if he thinks of one point, it is sufficient, instead of attempting to show all he knows about a topic. Mindmaps are a very useful technique here. Show him how to sketch out his answer and the points he wants to include before he starts to write his answer.

◆ If spelling is a problem, the student should use a vocabulary notebook in each subject. When the student comes across a new word, he should enter it into the notebook. Encourage the student to learn the spellings in this notebook. Use of multi-sensory teaching of spellings will help retention. This could involve the following steps

1. The student looks at the word picking out any difficult parts of the word.
2. He says the spelling.
3. He traces the spelling. If the student is asked to write the spelling out ten times, very often he will begin to spell the work incorrectly. Tracing means the word remains correct.
4. The student now writes the spelling from memory.
5. He checks if it is correct.
6. He then uses the word in a sentence.

♦ Encourage the student to use computers. Accept homework done in this format, as long as it is filed in an organised way. Computers can liberate the student with dyslexia. The only drawback to this is the fact that the student might not have the use of a computer in the state examinations as the numbers granted such an accommodation are quite low.

♦ Because the student with dyslexia can tend to be disorganised and lack structure in his work, he needs very clear guidelines and revision plans. Before an exam, write out the main headings of the material that will be examined, so he has a precise agenda. The clearer this is, the better. Allocate sections of work to particular weeks. Within a chapter, give the major headings for revision. These students benefit enormously from study skills workshops.

♦ Multi-sensory teaching can help learning. If lessons include written, oral and visual elements, these provide more 'hooks' for the student to remember the content.

♦ Write clearly on the board. Give him time to take down the information. A student with dyslexia may find this task difficult. Owing to poor memory skills, he takes down a smaller section of material than others each time he looks at the board and therefore has to look more frequently. He also may have difficulty finding his place when looking back at the board. He may also have difficulty deciphering script handwriting.

♦ Make sure the student has a 'picture' of the course being covered. When introducing new work, give an overview of the topic. It can help the student see the structure and can draw the different strands together for him.

♦ Check the readability of texts. Peer, in an article in the British Dyslexia Association Newsletter in 1996, described the Fogg Index which can be used to calculate the readability of texts. It can be calculated by looking at the average number of words in a sentence and the number of words with three syllables or more.

♦ Listen to what parents say about the student. Take into consideration their views on which teaching methods are successful. They have had the closest contact with the student and also may have to participate more often in homework than the parents of students without learning difficulties.

◆ Look for suggestions in the psychological assessment on what teaching strategies may work with the particular student.

◆ Besides listening to the student, parents and the psychologist about the most appropriate and successful approaches to learning and exams, the teacher also needs to develop his/her own ideas on what will work with the student.

It cannot be denied that meeting the needs of a student with dyslexia in the classroom will place enormous demands on the teacher who will need empathy, patience, extra time and imagination to present the courses in different ways. Many teachers are already stressed with the demands made upon them.

In justice, such students deserve that the school system is supportive of their needs and that their teachers, if they find the students cannot learn the way they normally teach, look for different methodologies to teach them the way they can learn. The thrust of the Education Act 1998 and the Task Force Report stresses the rights of the students for appropriate education. Subject teachers, who must meet the demands of the state exam system, realistically may find it difficult to give enough individual attention to one particular student who experiences learning difficulties. On the other hand, a teacher, who has an understanding of the dyslexia and adapts teaching strategies as much as possible, will do much for such students.

There is also a reward for the teacher when these students do achieve. Students with dyslexia can be enthusiastic learners when they find techniques that work for them. Since they are often of average or above-average intelligence and have only been held back by their verbal difficulties, they can make very good progress, which is hugely satisfying for the students, their parents and their teachers. With increasing confidence and new learning strategies, students with dyslexia can confound earlier predictions about their achievement.

Options after Junior Certificate

9

The ESRI publication *Issues in the Employment of School Leavers* (March 2000) highlights the fact that one in five young people continues to leave formal education before completion of the Leaving Certificate. The majority of these are absorbed into the workforce, generally into low pay, low skill and frequently temporary employment. It states that many young people who are entering the labour market do not have the skills or resources to maintain any long-term position in it. For those early school leavers who do obtain employment there are significant pay differentials in rates of pay between those who leave school with a Leaving Certificate and those who do not.

I would never advise students to leave school after their Junior Certificate unless they have plans that will further their qualifications and skills. It need not necessarily be a traditional Leaving Certificate. Options available include:

- Apprenticeships
- Youthreach
- Employment
- National Training and Development Institute Courses
- Leaving Certificate Traditional
- Leaving Certificate Applied
- Leaving Certificate Vocational

APPRENTICESHIPS

Apprenticeship is the route to becoming a skilled craftsperson. The apprentice works for an employer in a chosen occupation and learns the necessary skills and knowledge. Apprenticeships are standard-based. This means the apprentice has specific tests and assessments to ensure he meets certain pre-set standards of competency and skill. Apprenticeships comprise on-the-job training with the employer and off-the-job training in a FAS training centre or in an educational college.

The entry requirements for apprenticeships are that the applicant has reached 16 years of age and has obtained a D grade in five subjects at Junior Certificate level. Although Junior Certificate is the minimum requirement for entry, most apprentices actually have a Leaving Certificate.

There are three routes to an apprenticeship place:

◆ Some apprenticeships, such as the ESB, Aer Lingus, the Army and Aircorps, will be advertised in the national papers. If the apprenticeship is advertised in the national papers, the number of applicants rises. Apprenticeship places in state employment are normally advertised.

◆ Register with the local FAS office. It might have details of employers looking for apprenticeships

◆ Apply directly to local firms. The FAS office and the Golden Pages may help when compiling a list of firms.

If a student is offered an apprenticeship, it is important to check that it is a fully recognised apprenticeship, that the student will achieve certification at the end of the period and the firm will release him for off-the-job training. Also check that the student would be kept on for the full training period. Within two weeks of starting an apprenticeship, the apprentice should register with FAS. FAS actively encourages girls to apply for apprenticeship places including offering a bursary to employers.

RACE, Curragh House, Kildare, offers apprenticeship training for jockeys.

YOUTHREACH

Young people who leave school without any qualification or with a Junior Certificate only are the most vulnerable in the job market. Statistics show the highest unemployment and lowest wages are amongst this group. Youthreach is a special programme sponsored by the Department of Education and Science and the Department of Enterprise, Trade and Employment to give early school-leavers a second chance.

Youthreach offers young people an opportunity to gain qualifications and build self-confidence so they can move on into further education, training or work. It offers a range of qualifications including FETAC, City and Guilds, and Junior and Leaving Certificates. Youthreach is available in ninety FAS and VEC funded centres. The training and work experience lasts two years for those with no educational qualification and nineteen months for those with a Junior Certificate. Trainees receive regular FAS allowances depending on age.

EMPLOYMENT

While there is more employment available in recent years for students with no qualifications or with only their Junior Certificate, the work is mostly low wage employment, much of it part-time or temporary, with poor prospects of training or promotion.

NATIONAL TRAINING AND DEVELOPMENT INSTITUTE COURSES

The National Training and Development Institute (NTDI) is Ireland's largest non-Government training organisation with forty-six centres throughout Ireland catering for over 2000 students annually. There are no formal entry qualifications to any NTDI courses. Applicants must be over sixteen, be eligible for European Social Fund funding and be approved by the National Disability Authority. Applications from dyslexic students are considered for these courses

For the severely affected dyslexic student who is having enormous difficulty coping with the demands of second-level school, these courses provide a route to qualifications and skills. All the courses are certified by outside examination bodies.

LEAVING CERTIFICATE EXAMINATION

Since 1995 there are three types of Leaving Certificate being provided for students in senior cycle.

- The traditional Leaving Certificate. Here students do a two-year course of study and there is a final examination at the end of the two years. Most students take seven subjects. Subjects are offered at two levels, higher and ordinary. In Irish and Maths, foundation level is also offered. It would be expected that a student who did foundation level in these two subjects for Junior Certificate would take this level, as well as students who find the subjects exceptionally difficult at senior level. *Foundation level Maths and Irish are not acceptable for entry to the majority of CAO courses.* The entry requirement for the vast majority of certificate courses in the Institutes of Technology is the student should have five subjects in the Leaving Certificate including a D in English or Irish and in Maths. A decision that a student should take foundation level Maths might be made in second year. The student and his parents often may not realise that the consequence of this decision which is that the student is not eligible for the Institutes of Technology courses after Leaving Certificate.

- Leaving Certificate Applied Programme (LCAP). This is a two year self-contained programme. Its objective is to prepare participants for adult and working life. It has three main elements:

  - Vocational preparation which focuses on the preparation for work, work experience, enterprise and communications.
  - Vocational education which gives students general life skills, including the arts, social education, leisure and languages.
  - General education which is concerned with the development of mathematical, information technology and practical skills necessary for specialist areas such as tourism, business, horticulture, engineering and technology.

    Students are assessed throughout the two years, they receive credit for completing modules of the course and there are exams at the end of the two years. After finishing the course, the students could go on to employment or to PLC courses. Since they have not sat a traditional Leaving Certificate examination, they will not be able to apply for

CAO courses directly as the points system does not apply to the LCAP. However a student could do a LCAP, go on to a PLC and then, on the basis of the PLC qualification, apply to the Institutes of Technology through the CAO system. The LCAP was offered for the first time in 1996 in about sixty schools. By 2002 approximately 300 hundred schools were offering it. The Department of Education and Science has details of schools where it is offered.

♦ Leaving Certificate Vocational Programme (LCVP). The objective of this programme is to strengthen the vocational dimension of the Leaving Certificate through relating and integrating specific pairings of subjects. There are link modules to increase the vocational focus of the Leaving Certificate. The student takes a minimum of five subjects and these include Irish and a foreign language. Subjects which complement one another are grouped together and the student takes a particular group of subjects e.g. Engineering and Technical Drawing, Home Economics and Biology. There are link modules covering preparation for work, work experience and enterprise education. As the student sits the Leaving Certificate examination he can apply to CAO at the end of the LCVP. LCVP was available in over 150 schools in 1996 and by 2002 the number had risen to over 500. The Department of Education and Science has the list of schools offering it. If the student is interested in applying for CAO, check if the LCVP course has five or six Leaving Certificate subjects. Six subjects are counted for points so taking five subjects may put the student at a disadvantage. The Nursing Application Centre and the Gardai accept the work experience and enterprise education module as a Leaving Certificate subject. When applying to the Institutes of Technology, a pass grade in the link module is worth 30 points, a merit grade 50 points and a distinction grade 70 points.

In my view unless there are particular circumstances, the preferable option for the vast majority of students is a Leaving Certificate of some type, apprenticeship or, if appropriate, a NTDI course. The other options do not provide the same level of opportunity.

SUBJECT CHOICE FOR SENIOR CYCLE

This is a key moment in career choice for students. In Ireland, because students may take seven subjects or more for the Leaving Certificate, it is still possible to leave many paths open and not narrow one's options after the Junior Certificate. This is generally a good thing as it gives students time to mature before making critical career decisions. In the U.K. this is the time when students specialise and take a narrow range of subjects for A levels.

However, in Ireland where such a wide range of subjects is offered, option structures may be restricted and students with dyslexia may be at a disadvantage. They may have to take subjects that are verbally based and they may not be able to specialise in their best subjects. As an example of this, take a student with dyslexia who is very proficient in the Maths, Business and Technical subjects. This student may have to take English, Irish and a third language as three of his seven subjects. Unless the option structure is very open, it is possible he may have to take other verbally based subjects such as Economics or History. If the same student could choose subjects such as English, Maths, Physics, Chemistry, Accounting, Technical Graphics and Engineering, it would certainly improve his chances of maximising points for the CAO system as well as giving him subjects he may enjoy studying.

I have always enjoyed working with students as they face the challenge of choosing senior cycle options. It is a time when one sees the adult emerging in the student as he faces up to making major decisions. Some students can be very mature and have very clear ideas, so subject choice is relatively simple. Others, while they have begun to think about careers, are not ready to narrow their options. It is important that these students do not limit their choice of careers. The Leaving Certificate provides a structure for students to maintain a wide choice. If a student is taking Irish (unless exempt), English and Maths and chooses a language (unless NUI exemption is in place), a science and a business subject among his options, most careers and courses are open to him.

At this stage, when the student is making choices, parents and students need information on careers and course requirements. This is the time to start a careers file and begin research on colleges and courses. It is necessary to know the requirements for courses.

There are two sets of requirements:

◆ Colleges set minimum entry requirements. An example of this is the Institutes of Technology which set a requirement of five subjects in the Leaving Certificate with a pass grade in Maths and English or Irish for many of their courses. The four Colleges of NUI (UCC, UCD, UCG, and Maynooth) specify six subjects, two at Higher level, with a pass in English, Irish and a third language. Chapter 3 contains information on possible exemptions from these requirements. Trinity College Dublin and Limerick University require the student to have English and another language as an entry requirement.

◆ Certain courses have specific entry requirements. These are often related to what the student will be studying, e.g. a course in languages will specify that a student will need a certain grade in that language at Leaving Certificate.

Some examples of subject requirements include:

Maths	Higher level Maths is essential for Engineering degrees and Actuarial studies. Ordinary level Maths is a minimum requirement for many Institute of Technology courses.
English	Higher level English is essential for Clinical Speech in TCD, Journalism in DCU and Communications in DCU. Ordinary level English is required for a wide range of Institute of Technology courses.
Irish	Higher level Irish is essential for Primary Teacher training. Ordinary level Irish is required for entry in NUI colleges unless the student has an exemption.
Science	Science courses will require a science subject. TCD requires two sciences for some medical/ paramedical courses. DIT requires higher level Chemistry for Dietetics.

Complete information on course requirements is available in the College brochures. These are available from the Admissions Office in each college.

The criteria for choosing subjects for Leaving Certificate should include:

- The student has the essential subjects needed for the courses he may consider doing after Leaving Certificate.
- He chooses subjects which will be of interest to him and that he will enjoy. This will help with motivation. Logically these subjects would tally with the strengths shown in his profile of abilities.
- If he is interested in applying for courses in the CAO system, he chooses subjects that will give him the best exam grades to maximise his points.

Developing a Learning Style

10

Most of the content of this book concentrates on how parents, teachers, school administration and support services can help the student with dyslexia. The student needs, as he grows older, to develop ways to help him become an independent learner. It is a key step if he is to achieve his potential. This chapter looks at ways to achieve this. It is based on an article that I wrote after the 1999 AGM of the Dyslexia Association. For the first time students with dyslexia were invited to attend and given a forum for the exchange of views. From the resulting discussion it appeared many of them did not know exactly how dyslexia affected them and what were the most appropriate learning strategies. Some of this confusion is explained by the fact that dyslexia affects each student differently. The assessment can be used to help the student understand how dyslexia affects him personally, and what are his strengths and weaknesses. The most appropriate learning strategies will depend on these. It is up to the student to test out the possible strategies and decide what works best for him. Below is a list of suggestions for the student to consider.

It is addressed directly at the third-level student, but many of the suggestions are equally applicable to the second-level student, particularly in senior cycle.

ORGANISATION OF TIME, WORK AND WORKPLACE

- ◆ Timetable. Have a structured timetable for study from the first day of a course, so steady progress is made. It is more difficult for the student with dyslexia to cram before an exam. It can lead to confusion and feeling of being overwhelmed.

- Regular time of day. Check which part of the day suits you best for study. Some students find morning the most beneficial, some the evening. Consider the foods and drinks that might affect concentration such as coffee. Lack of food can also do this.
- Set a given period of time, not too long. Students with dyslexia often have to concentrate harder than other students. If you work for too long, your work and/or concentration may deteriorate and mistakes multiply. For the same reason, try to avoid study when rushed, under pressure or tired.
- Set out realistic study goals and priorities.
- Keep only one diary for all appointments, dates, exams, assignments, projects, social life, and work commitments. A personal organiser such as a Psion may be useful.
- Study at a desk, in a comfortable chair and comfortable clothes with a quiet environment.

FINDING HELP

- Talk to the academic staff and disability support staff in the institution about the support services and your needs.
- Seek assistance from a counsellor, tutor or mentor who could help you develop strategies for learning more effectively. Do this when the course begins and don't wait until you are in trouble and overwhelmed by the demands of the course.
- Ask the following be given to you in writing:
  - Booklists, course outlines and a schedule of assignment dates.
  - Timetables, later changes in the timetable and exam timetable.
  - Guidelines on how to present out assignments, bibliographies, footnotes, etc.
  - Feedback on completed assignments.
  - Practice exam questions that demonstrate exam format.
- Join or form a co-operative learning group on subjects for topics studied.
- Ask someone to proofread essays or projects before handing them up. It would be useful if such work was discussed with a

tutor prior to preliminary drafting and that the early assignments are checked by a tutor prior to submission. Such supports are available in some colleges.

♦ Sometimes the student may encounter a lecturer who is not aware of the range of difficulties that a student with dyslexia may have. Be prepared and have information on the topic ready to hand out and then be ready to explain how you are affected.

STUDY METHODS

♦ Become computer literate as soon as possible, preferably early on at second-level. By the time you reach third-level, your computer skills should be excellent. You may find it easier to study lecture notes that have been entered on a computer, the print being more legible than handwriting. Do you have the skills to use a laptop in lectures? Will lecturers give you permission to do so? If not, enter the notes on the computer the same evening as the lecture, when the notes are still fresh in your mind.

♦ Check if assistive technology can help you. Read Chapter 6 on such technology.

♦ Do prescribed reading in advance so you are prepared for lectures. It will make you familiar with main topics and key words and will prevent spelling new vocabulary a major problem.

♦ Sit in the front of the room where visual and auditory are clearer and it is easier to concentrate on the content of the lecture.

♦ Attend every class, tutorial, and laboratory session. Much of your learning will result from the lecture presentation where learning can be facilitated by the visual, aural, and written elements. Students with dyslexia usually have more difficulty catching up on missed lectures from other students' notes that are only in written form.

♦ If taking notes by hand, ensure you take down the main points and structure of what a lecturer is saying. Use mindmaps, or headings, sub headings and points. Leave plenty of space, so you can expand on points later. If a lecturer uses a word you cannot spell, write it phonically and circle or mark it. This means you will not waste time wondering how to spell it and lose the thread of the lecture. Listen carefully to the opening remarks of the lecturer. A good lecturer will state the purpose of the lecture and will sum up at the end. He may also give clear guidelines that help with notes such as enumerating the number of points he is going to make. If your handwriting is difficult to read, perhaps ask a fellow-student to take a carbon copy or photocopy his notes. Don't miss the lecture if you are doing this.

- Ask a lecturer prior to the lecture for the notes or a copy of the overhead slides he will be using. It means less writing and you can listen and concentrate on what is said. The structure and sequence of the lecture will be clearly laid out. It is also possible to include additional notes or points where relevant.
- Tape lectures (with prior permission). You can concentrate on listening to the lecture to understand it and use the tape to make notes that evening. You will need a good mike to cut out background noise and sit at the front of the room. Label the tape clearly. It may provide a welcome break from reading to listen to such work.
- Transcribe or refine notes as soon as possible after a lecture to ensure they are legible and structured and that you understand the points in them.
- Write down questions or points not understood for discussion later with the tutor or lecturer.
- Develop a shorthand for keywords which help to minimise writing, e.g. envr for environment.
- Ask lecturers to shorten booklists so that the essential texts are clearly marked.
- Ensure you understand the essay, project, or assessment requirements before you start.
- Use a reader service or ask to have essential texts audio-taped.

SPECIFIC STRATEGIES
Students who learn aurally
If you learn more through aural than from written information, think of using tapes of lectures, taping notes, and find out if any of your texts are available on tape. Get involved in discussions of topics with lecturers and fellow students. Repeat material to be learnt aloud. Read drafts of essays aloud to see if they make sense.

Students who learn visually
Some students have a strong visual memory. This can be used when learning. Such students will be able to recall the look of a page of notes. This assists in the recall of the content of the page. Make use of colour, numbering of points, margins, headings and diagrams when making notes. Mindmaps will be very useful here. The Careers-World website at www.careersworld.com has information on mindmaps.

Difficulty with text
Some students may have difficulty in deciphering the meaning of complex texts. They may have to reread pages several times. This may as a result of the number of clauses in each sentence or new vocabulary. Ask for help and direction. Ask that reading lists highlight the essential texts to be read. Always know your purpose in reading a text. Make notes showing the development of the points in the text. Reading the text aloud may help in comprehension. If the type is very small, have it enlarged. Do your reading early in the day, as if you are tired , it can become more difficult to concentrate.

The Kurzweil 3000 is a computer programme that scans text and reads aloud. This could be particularly useful.

Spelling
If spelling difficulties remain, develop your ability to cope. Ask others to proofread documents. Use the spell check on the computer or a Franklin word master. Keep a list of new words and learn them off by heart. Inform the academic staff of the difficulties and give examples of your spelling. Ask that your examiners be informed of

the difficulties. In a number of courses spelling might be critical to achievement, e.g. medical or paramedical courses where the correct spelling of drugs or conditions is needed or in teaching where the student will be expected to be able to spell correctly before a class. In these cases it will be necessary to develop spelling strategies for accuracy. Gilroy & Miles in *Dyslexia at College* have a useful chapter on this topic.

Memory Difficulties

Some students find it difficult to retain information over time. Strategies that might help include:

- Good note taking skills so the notes are clear and comprehensible.
- Learning the notes. Some students feel that once the notes are made and filed, that the work is done. Notes must be learnt. This learning can be checked by an oral recital or writing them out again. Mnemonics may help with learning.
- A revision plan where the topic is revised on a frequent basis. Such a plan could entail learning the material on the night of the lecture, a weekly revision of all new material learnt, and a monthly revision of the month's work. Each time you revise it will take a shorter time.
- Make sure you understand what you are learning, as this makes it easier to memorise.

Options after Leaving Certificate

11

Here again it is obvious from statistics that the longer the student remains in education the greater are the opportunities open to him. The ESRI survey published in 1999 on the Economic Status of School-leavers shows that expanding economy has provided an increase in employment for school-leavers with Leaving Certificate qualifications since 1994. In 1998 the unemployment rate for such students was averaging 5%. The survey also showed how the results in the Leaving Certificate affect employment opportunities. The unemployment rate was 5.9% for school leavers with 5 D grades in the Leaving Certificate. It was down to 2.7% for students with four C grades on higher papers.

The choices available after Leaving Certificate have improved for all students including the student with dyslexia. There are more jobs, new courses, more places on courses, new routes to qualifications and the provision of more support services. It is a rapidly changing sector of education. Although it is often suggested that there is a shortage of places on courses for students after Leaving Certificate, this is not the reality. There are a limited number of places on certain high demand courses such as Medicine, Law, Veterinary and Pharmacy. This scarcity of places raises the points for these courses. However there are plenty of places on courses available for school-leavers after the Leaving Certificate.

In 2001 close to 60,000 students sat the Leaving Certificate. There were approximately 34,000 places available in the CAO system. There were another 17,000 places available in the PLC system. So, between the PLC and CAO systems, there were places in further education for over 75% of the Leaving Certificate group. This does not include the other application systems open to students such as

CERT, Teagasc, and the U.K. colleges.

There are new routes to qualifications. PLC courses can lead on to certificate and diploma courses which can then lead on to degree courses. In 2001 over 2000 places on courses in the Institutes of Technology were reserved for students from the PLC sector. The courses covered the full spectrum of courses from art and design to business, from science and computers to engineering. Students and their parents need to research widely so that they are informed about all the choices open to them.

The opportunities available in the CAO system are not only for students who get several honours in the Leaving Certificate. There were approximately one hundred and sixty courses at certificate level in the Institutes of Technology in 2001 that were offered at 200 points or below. This equates to a Leaving Certificate with one or two honours or high grades in pass subjects. Over fifty courses were offered to all qualified applicants. This means students with 5 'D's on Ordinary level papers including English and Maths would qualify for a place.

I know of a student with a one honour Leaving Certificate, who studied for the Certificate in Electronic Engineering, went on to do a Diploma in Electronic Engineering, transferred to Limerick University to obtain a degree and finished by doing a Master's. While this is rare, it is possible and the system is flexible enough for students to go as far as their abilities allow. This opens opportunities to the student with dyslexia. The student may not obtain the points to get on a degree course from his Leaving Certificate results, perhaps due to the number of verbally based subjects he has to take. He may obtain a place on a certificate level course. When he is studying a specialised topic which capitalises on his natural abilities, he may find it possible to progress to diploma and degree levels.

The main routes for a student seeking qualifications after Leaving Certificate are:

◆ The Central Applications Office (CAO): courses at degree, diploma and certificate level in Universities, Institutes of Technology, Nursing, and other colleges.

- Post Leaving Certificate courses (PLCs).
- UCAS, the U.K. application system.
- Colleges of Further Education in the U.K.
- CERT, hotel, catering and tourism courses.
- Teagasc, agriculture and horticulture courses.
- FAS, apprenticeships and training courses.

THE CENTRAL APPLICATIONS OFFICE (CAO)

This is the main application system for Leaving Certificate students. It covers approximately 34,000 places on courses in forty-six colleges and forty-one schools of nursing. It is a joint application system for degree, diploma and certificate level courses. The courses offered are in the universities, institutes of technology, nursing and some of the private colleges. It is important to remember that fees are payable for courses in private colleges although tax relief can be claimed.

It is a single application form. The student can apply for up to ten degree courses and ten certificate/diploma courses, a total of twenty courses. If the student is interested in nursing there are a further three lists of ten choices under the headings of general, psychiatric or mental handicap.

The CAO handbook sets out the precise application procedures to be followed and is available from the CAO from October. The important dates to remember are the closing date, 1st February and late closing date 1st May. If the student wishes to change his order of preference on the list of courses or to introduce new courses, there is a change of mind facility up to 1st July. There are a small number of courses that have additional selection procedures, such as aptitude tests or portfolios. These courses must be included prior to 1st February and it is not possible to introduce these courses on a change-of-mind slip. Offers of places are determined by points for the vast majority of courses provided the student satisfies the college entry requirements and any specified course requirements. Details of the points system are in Fig. 11.1. The points from the previous year can be used as a rough guide when looking at courses but the points are set each year by the number of places on the course and the number of applicants.

The points system			
Leaving Certificate grade	Higher level	Ordinary level	Bonus
A1	100	60	40
A2	90	50	35
B1	85	45	30
B2	80	40	25
B3	75	35	20
C1	70	30	15
C2	65	25	10
C3	60	20	5
D1	55	15	
D2	50	10	
D3	45	5	

The best six results are counted for points calculation. Bonus points for Higher Maths are awarded by the University of Limerick.

Fig. 11.1 *The Points System*

I am not going to explain the precise details of the CAO system. Such information is contained in the CAO handbook. However there are some points relevant to students with dyslexia.

◆ It is very important that decisions about colleges and courses are thoroughly researched. The student should collect relevant college brochures, attend open days, talk to the staff at the colleges and to students attending the courses. It means reading the brochures and knowing the content of the courses in which the student is interested. The same course title can differ in content from college to college. An example of this is the National Certificate in Business Studies. In some colleges it includes the study of a language and in others it does not.

◆ The structure of the course can be important for the student with dyslexia. Continuous assessment is a system where assignments are graded throughout the year and form part of the final assessment. Semesters mean that the year's work can be broken into two halves and examined separately. Both continuous assessment and semesters can help the student with dyslexia, by spreading the academic burden throughout the year and reducing the amount to be memorised for an exam. Some courses in certain disciplines are taught through lectures and practicals, where the student can apply the knowledge gained. This hand-on experience provides multi-sensory teaching that can help the student with dyslexia. Other courses may be taught through lectures and reading lists. This may pose greater difficulty for the student, who may need help in reducing the reading list to the essential texts.

◆ Use the CAO system fully. This means applying for the twenty courses allowed between both lists (not including Nursing). **It is important that choices be in order of preference the entire way down each list.** Do not restrict the choice to one location. It is a very noticeable trend that Dublin students do not apply on a national basis but tend to apply to Dublin colleges only. They place themselves at a disadvantage in so doing. The points for courses in Dublin are usually higher than for the same course outside the Dublin area. Take the case of a student interested in Electronics. At degree level in 2001 the points ranged from 480 for Engineering in UCG to 330 for an Electronic Engineering degree in Waterford. At certificate level, the points ranged from 255 for Applied Electronics in DIT to courses where all qualified applicants (those with five passes including English and Maths) got places. On the both the degree list and the certificate/diploma list the student should put the courses he wants in order of preference. This is the most important instruction in filling in the form. He could then use his ninth and tenth preference on each list for courses he may consider if his Leaving Certificate results are lower than he expects. For example, he may want to do an engineering degree in Dublin and will list these courses among his top preferences. He may then consider including courses with lower points as a lower preference. On the certificate/diploma list the student should put the courses he wants in order of preference but again use the ninth and tenth choices for courses that need fewer points.

◆ Points do not give a ranking to how good a course is. They are a reflection of the number of students applying for that particular course in a particular year. Remember points will vary from year to year but there are patterns to be seen. One pattern is that students prefer to take a course in large cities that have a thriving student population. In the case of the National Certificate in Computing, the same qualification is offered in many of the Institutes of Technology. The student may need more points to get a place in Dublin, Cork or Galway and yet the student who studies in other colleges will obtain the same qualification. The points for certain types of courses may reflect the perception that students hold of employment prospects after the course. An example of such a trend is engineering degree courses where the points requirement dropped during the 1980's and have risen sharply in the 1990's. More recently in 2002 the number of applications for computer courses dropped due to the cut back of employment in that industry.

◆ Even if the student feels confident about obtaining a CAO place, he could also apply to PLC courses as a precaution. He can turn down courses in September but he may not be able to apply for them at this stage. So the student should apply for a PLC with the idea that if he does not get a CAO place, he could do a PLC course. It may be possible to apply to CAO the following year using his PLC results.

◆ The CAO structure is very flexible at certificate/diploma level. Students can do a two-year certificate in the Institutes of Technology. If they obtain the necessary results they can do one more year and get a diploma. It is now possible to do a further year of study after the diploma to obtain a degree qualification. The CAO handbook indicates courses that have add-on diplomas and degrees.

◆ It might also be possible to transfer to university after completing a national certificate or diploma. The transfer is based on the student's results but it applies to certain faculties only, such as Business Studies, Computing, Science and Engineering.

◆ ACCS is a system which allows part-time students acquire nationally recognised qualifications in the Institutes of Technology. This can provide another route to qualifications.

SUPPORT SERVICES FOR STUDENTS AT THIRD-LEVEL

In recent years colleges at third-level have become more aware of dyslexia and the difficulties faced by students with dyslexia. In my opinion there has been much more development in support services at this level than at second-level. This development of services has been supported by the work of AHEAD (Association for Higher Education Access and Disability). Students with dyslexia represent the fastest growing group of students with disabilities in higher education. AHEAD held a conference in Trinity College in 1999 called *Dyslexia and Third-level Education in Ireland –Future Directions.* Delegates were presented with models of good practice in the areas of admissions policies, psychological assessment facilities, personal counselling and support and advocacy services for students with dyslexia. The proceedings are published on the AHEAD website www.ahead.ie. The Conference was a significant development in beginning to formulate policy at institutional and national level on dyslexia in higher education. Prof. P. Pumfrey stated at the conference 'No country can afford the waste that occurs when high ability is obscured by the adverse and cumulative effects of dyslexia on a student's attainment and motivation'.

Nearly all higher level colleges have Disability Support Officers or Access Officers who give help, advice and support to students with special needs. The institutions are anxious to make appropriate provision for such students in good time. Details on how to use this procedure are given in the CAO handbook. The student ticks the box marked 'Medical/Physical Condition/Specific Learning Difficulty' on page one of application form. The CAO will then contact the student to obtain further details and will supply these to the relevant Institutions. The provision of such information does not adversely affect the application in any way. The support services provided by colleges may include:

- A waiver of minimum educational requirements for entry for certain courses. The NUI exemption from the 3rd language requirement is an example.
- Direct application to the College.
- Latitude in the points requirement for courses.
- Access of photocopying.
- Access to psychological assessment if it is thought the student has undiagnosed dyslexia.
- Copies of lecturer's notes.
- Study skills tutorials.
- Assistance with reading lists to identify key texts.
- One-to-one tutorial system.
- In-service or information circulated to staff on dyslexia.
- Extra time in exams.
- Support Services in exams such as scribes, readers, taping and use of computers.
- Lecturers informed of student's difficulties.
- Examiners informed of student's difficulties.
- Use of assistive technology such as word processors, voice recognition software, scanners to read text, programmes such as TextHELP.

Some Colleges have very specific help for students with dyslexia. Examples of this include: UCC and Tralee IT both have a dedicated dyslexia tutor. Dun Laoghaire Institute of Art, Design and Technology and the National College of Art and Design both have a writing and research skills service for students. Students and/or their parents should ring relevant colleges and talk to the Disability Support Officer to ascertain the exact services provided in the college and how to access them.

It is extremely useful to have a recent assessment that indicates the supports the student needs. The student should discuss with the psychologist, parents and/or second level teachers the supports that facilitate his learning styles, so that he is in the position to be able to articulate his needs when asked. He should have thought through the supports that are useful for him, both when studying and when taking exams. The Disability Support Services are there to facilitate the student but they do need clear information coming from the assessment and the student about the necessary supports. This reflects the fact that each student with dyslexia has a unique profile of strengths and weaknesses.

POST LEAVING CERTIFICATE COURSES

This is a rapidly developing sector of education. Each year more courses are added to the list and existing courses are further developed. These developments include links to other educational institutions both here and in Britain. While the vast majority of these courses is aimed at the Ordinary level Leaving Certificate student who is unlikely to get a CAO place, some have such a high reputation that they could be a student's first option regardless of the CAO place offered.

They are primarily designed to prepare students for the world of work and to develop vocational skills. They provide access to employment, further study and further training. It is possible for students who have successfully completed PLC courses to obtain a place on certificate level courses in the CAO system. PLC courses are available in a wide variety of colleges throughout the country. There is a list of main PLC colleges in Appendix B.

Students must apply individually to each college. There is no centralised system. Many of the colleges have open days usually in February and March each year. Applications will be accepted from January onwards or at the open days. Closing dates also can vary. Some, particularly for courses with a high demand for places, can be as early as March. However there can be places available on some courses as late as September.

The selection procedures differ and may include interviews, aptitude tests or the presentation of a portfolio. Some courses are in very high demand, particularly where the college is running a unique course such as the Colaiste Dhulaigh Communications course or the Ballyfermot Senior College Animation course. The most common selection procedure is an interview. A portfolio will be needed when applying for Art and Design courses. For Communication, Radio and TV courses, relevant experience which may form part of a portfolio is desirable. For Journalism, a portfolio of published material is useful.

Since it can be an interview system, this may suit the student with dyslexia who may not have very good grades in the Leaving Certificate but who is articulate and who has gained relevant experience. After Junior Certificate, the student should begin to develop his C.V. Work experience, achievements in sport, contribution to the community and award schemes such as An Gaisce (the President's Award Scheme), all can help at interview.

There is a vast range of courses in this sector. Some are available at many of the PLC colleges, some are unique to one college. They can be classified into main groups as follows:

Art, Craft, Design	Art, Craft, Design, Fashion Design, Interior Design, Computer Aided Design,Furniture Restoration, Animation.
Business	Business, Secretarial, Computer Applications, Marketing, Languages, Retail Studies,Auctioneering, Security.
Science, Technology and Natural Resources	Laboratory Techniques, Horticulture, Motor Technology, Food Science, Construction, Electronics Technology, Equestrian Studies.
Services, Leisure and Tourism	Hotel, Catering, Tourism, Beauty, Child Care, Nursing Studies, Hairdressing, Tennis Coaching, Marine Skills, Leisure Management, Football, Heritage Studies.
Communications, Drama	Advertising, Journalism, Communications, Video Production, Performing Arts, Languages.

FETAC, (the Further Education and Training Awards Council) has been set up to provide a certification system, to determine standards and to evaluate the quality of programmes. In the past a wide variety of Bodies/Institutes has acted as certifying organisations. FETAC replaced the NCVA and it is hoped it will bring greater coherence to the system. FETAC makes awards at four levels. Most PLC courses are offered at Level 2. The standards of certification apply nationally. This standardisation will facilitate mobility between different educational levels and allow integration with European systems of vocational qualifications.

The Institutes of Technology recognise and give credit for FETAC Level 2 courses. In 2001 approximately 2,000 places on certificate level courses were reserved for students with FETAC Level 2 qualifications covering the entire spectrum from Art and Design to Business and from Science and Computers to Engineering. Applicants for these places apply on pages 3 & 4 of the CAO form. Places are allocated on the results of the PLC course. Each PLC course has eight modules. These include five vocational modules, two general studies modules (one of which must be Communications) and one work experience module. The grade-point average over the eight modules of the PLC course will decide how places are allocated when applying to the CAO.

Besides the FETAC certification, some courses have recognition from professional bodies such as the Professional Accountancy Bodies or they receive certification from organisations such as City and Guilds. Some courses award British Higher National Diplomas. Some courses allow the student, after successfully completing the PLC, to transfer to a British University.

These courses have been designed to prepare students for the world of work. On completing the course, students can take different routes such as:

◆ Go directly into the labour market.
◆ Continue in education through a CAO application to Institutes of Technology.
◆ Continue in education through the U.K. system. Some PLC courses have already established a direct link to further qualification with British universities.

Usually there are no course fees, although examination and administration fees may have to be paid. Maintenance grants are paid to students. These grants are means tested.

COLLEGES IN THE UK SYSTEM

There is a centralised application system in the UK for both degree and diploma places at university. It is for all the universities. It is called UCAS (University and College Admissions Service).

The closing date for applications is 15th December, except in the case of Oxford and Cambridge universities when the closing date is 15th October. Students fill in the form and list up to six courses. These courses are not in order of preference (except for Art and Design courses). The system differs from the CAO in that personal information is included on the form. On a page included as part of the form, the student can state his reasons for choosing these courses, his relevant work experience, relevant school subjects and his achievements. The form is passed on to an academic referee, usually a designated teacher in school, who writes a confidential reference on the student covering points such as ability, achievement, potential, contribution to school life, any disability and a forecast of Leaving Certificate results. The referee posts the form to UCAS.

UCAS sends a copy of the form to each college to which the student applied. Each college considers the application and may make a conditional offer. The conditional offer will specify the academic goals to be achieved in the Leaving Certificate. The student will know in March or April what results he will need to achieve in the Leaving Certificate to ensure his place on a course. The academic goals set out in each offer may differ depending on the demand for places on the particular course in that college. While the student may receive six offers, he can accept two only. The student may choose a college which has set high academic goals in the Leaving Certificate as a firm acceptance and hold a lower offer as insurance in case he does not get the results he hopes for in the Leaving Certificate

For degree level courses, colleges generally look for four Leaving Certificate honours subjects as a minimum qualification. For diploma courses the minimum entry qualifications may be less. Courses are offered at levels much above this minimum qualification, depending on the course, the university and the geographical location of the college.

Applicants who live in the EU must pay towards the tuition fees for each year of the course (£1075 sterling in 2001/2002). Students, who are eligible for Irish Higher Education maintenance grants, can avail of these grants while they attend most courses in the U.K. There are some exceptions to this, so be careful to check that the courses chosen are eligible. Irish Higher Education grants are means-tested.

There are over 80,000 courses in the UCAS system which include subjects and subject combinations not available here. There is no change of mind facility as there is in the CAO system. This means there is a greater need for detailed research before filling in the form. Students need to know as much as possible about the courses and colleges to which they are applying. Since applications are submitted in October/December prior to the Leaving Certificate, this research should be started during fifth year.

Reasons why students with dyslexia may consider applying to the U.K.:

- ◆ Although for high demand courses such as Law, Medicine, Veterinary and Pharmacy entry standards are as high in the U.K. as they are in Ireland, the entrance standards on more general courses such as Computers, Business Studies, Languages and Engineering may be lower than the equivalent course on the CAO system. One reason for this is the different population structure. In Ireland there is more demand for college places because of the very high proportion of young people in our population.

- ◆ The support services for students with dyslexia were developed earlier in the UK. However there has been huge progress in Ireland in the provision of supports for students at third-level.

- ◆ There is a wider range of courses and options within courses available in the U.K.

- ◆ The Irish application procedure does not allow for information about the student to be included unless one applies as a nonstandard applicant by ticking the Medical/Physical/Specific Learning Difficulty box on the CAO form. The U.K. procedure allows for other information both in the student's personal statement and the academic reference. The decision to make an offer takes this information into account. This could be of benefit to a student with dyslexia.

◆ Many Irish applicants use the U.K. system as a form of insurance in case they do not get the place they want in Ireland.

Other sources of information on the U.K. system include:

◆ The British Council in Dublin will answer queries on U.K. courses.

◆ Philomena Ott's book *How to detect and manage Dyslexia* contains a detailed chapter on further and higher education in the U.K.

◆ SKILL is an organisation in the U.K. similar to AHEAD in Ireland which is concerned about the needs of students with disabilities. It has many publications which could be helpful.

◆ There is a CD Rom called Ecctis, which is a database of all the courses in the UCAS system. It is available in some schools and Youth Information Offices.

◆ In September each year the Institute of Guidance Counsellors, in conjunction with the Irish Times, organise the Higher Options Conference in the R.D.S., Dublin. Many British colleges as well as Irish colleges are represented. It is advisable that students attend this conference. It is held over three days. An information night for parents is held during the conference.

COLLEGES OF FURTHER EDUCATION IN UK

These are colleges all over the U.K. offering diploma or certificate level qualifications in the fields of Engineering, Computer, Business, Social Care, Art, Catering, Leisure or Teaching. Contact the colleges individually to see the application procedure.

Nursing

There are approximately training places available annually in the nursing schools. Application is made through the CAO system. Information about nursing in Ireland is available from An Bord Altranais.

The entry requirements for nursing are:

- Applicants must be 17 years old on 1st June in the year they apply. Six subjects in the Leaving Certificate are needed, two of which must be Grade C3 or higher on the honours paper and four at Grade D3 or higher on the ordinary level paper. Subjects should include English, Maths, Irish (unless exempt by the Department of Education) and a science subject. Foundation level Maths and Irish are not acceptable

There are three types of nurse training available in Ireland.

- General nursing is concerned with the provision of total nursing care for the sick and physically injured.
- Psychiatric Nursing is concerned with caring for people with psychiatric illnesses.
- Mental handicapped nursing concerned with children and adults with a mental handicap.

There are many pre-nursing courses and childcare courses available in the PLC sector. Check out local colleges (Appendix B). The pre-nursing course gives relevant work experience and information about nursing. Students still need the minimum Leaving Certificate requirements. Some PLC courses allow the option of doing some Leaving Certificate subjects in conjunction with the pre-nursing course. This would be of benefit to a student who did not obtain the necessary grades for entry to nursing in the Leaving Certificate.

There is a dental nursing course in the Dental Hospital in TCD. Applications are made directly to the college. Veterinary nursing is available through UCD.

Hotel, catering and Tourism courses

CERT is the state training agency for hotels, catering and tourism. It advertises application procedures and closing dates for courses in January each year

For most courses students need to be seventeen and to have passed their Leaving Certificate.

CERT provide courses for the following:

◆ Chef
◆ Accommodation Assistant
◆ Waiter/Waitress
◆ Hospitality Assistant
◆ Bartender
◆ Tourism Assistant
◆ Reception Skills
◆ Travel Agency Skills

There are nine courses in hotel and catering management provided through the CAO system at degree, diploma and certificate level. Ballyfermot Senior College has a PLC course in hotel management. The Northern Ireland Hotel and Catering College, Portrush, runs a variety of hotel and catering courses.

AGRICULTURE

Teagasc offers a range of agricultural and horticultural courses throughout the country. The qualifications are accredited by HETAC and FETAC.

Courses offered include:

◆ The National Certificate in Agriculture
◆ The National Diploma in Horticulture
◆ The Vocational Certificate in Agriculture
◆ The Vocational Certificate in Horticulture
◆ The Vocational Certificate in Forestry
◆ The Vocational Certificate in Horsebreeding and Training.
◆ Farm Management Training
◆ Trainee Farmer Scheme

Further information on these courses is available from Teagasc. Applications for the first two courses are on the CAO, otherwise applications are made directly to the colleges.

FAS TRAINING COURSES

Apprenticeship training has been dealt with Chapter 9. FAS also, through its training centre network, provides close on 170 different training courses of an industrial and commercial nature for unemployed workers, those wishing to update their skills or change their careers and for school-leavers unable to obtain employment.

FAS courses are available to men and women who are unemployed, redundant or out of full-time education. All applicants for FAS courses must register with their local FAS employment services offices.

Training allowances are paid to trainees. Accommodation costs are subsidised for those who must live away from home during the course. For further information, contact the local FAS employment services offices or training centre.

FAS, in conjunction with DAI, run a course called 'Career Paths for Dyslexia'(FAS course code BA58F). It is the only course in Ireland catering for the specific needs of adults with dyslexia. It is run in Celbridge, Co. Kildare. The duration of the course is six months. The course content includes: Health and Safety, Presentation Techniques, Interviewing Techniques, Capacity Building, Personal Development, Information Technology, Literacy Skills, Business Planning, and a placement.

Choosing a Career Direction

Students are better equipped for the job market if they have further training or education after the Leaving Certificate. This is why the major decision for the students in their last year at second-level is the courses they should apply for to continue their education.

There is rapid change and developments in the courses provided after the Leaving Certificate. Sometimes in speaking to parents, I am aware that their view of colleges and courses has remained fairly static since the time that they themselves were at school and they still hold the opinions about colleges and qualifications that they held then. This means they can lack an understanding of the complexities and the flexibility of the choices available now. Even as a guidance counsellor it is a major challenge to stay up-to-date with the constant innovation in the provision of courses. To be properly informed, parents need to make themselves aware of the major changes. Some of these changes include:

- ◆ The major contribution made by the Institutes of Technology. In some cases employers would look first to these colleges rather than the traditional universities because of the strength of the reputation of certain courses.
- ◆ The growth in add-on diplomas and degrees in the Institute of Technology sector. In the CAO handbook, such add-on qualifications are indicated in the lists of courses from each college.
- ◆ The growth in Post Leaving Certificate courses has been astronomical, both in the number and range of courses provided. Some courses are linked to degree courses in Britain.

In 2001, two thousand CAO places in the Institutes of Technology were reserved for students from the PLC sector.

♦ The increasing flexibility and adaptability of the system so students can move from Post Leaving Certificate course to national certificate, to national diploma and on to degree level. This provides alternative routes to qualifications.

♦ The introduction of systems such as ACCS to aid the part-time student acquire qualifications which are fully certified by the NCEA.

Because of the number of courses and alternative routes to qualifications, students and parents need to research courses. It is not something that should be left to sixth year. It can be difficult to make students realise the urgency to become informed about courses and to begin research. As a Guidance Counsellor, it is very frustrating to go through the CAO system in detail in the classroom in November and then to have some students wake up in mid-January and come and ask questions about the system when the closing date for applications is 1st February.

The first place to start the research is with the guidance counsellor in the school, who will be able to provide information about colleges, courses, open days and application procedures. The level of provision of a careers service can vary from school to school depending on whether there is a guidance counsellor and the number of hours that are allocated to guidance counselling. Since the guidance counsellor works within the school, he/she will have a good knowledge of the student's abilities, interests and possible results.

The development of the Internet has made access to information much more easy. The Colleges have each their own web site with information on the college and courses.

Further information can be gained from newspapers particularly around mid-August and mid-January. However there can an element of hyped-up information and headlines can tend to focus on courses where points have risen or the handful of courses that require 500 plus points. Outside the louder headlines, the papers do contain excellent information and sometimes information that is not available elsewhere. This is because of the rapid change in the nature of courses provided and in the job market itself. Publications tend to go out-of-date very quickly. These articles are often accompanied by large advertisements about colleges and courses. Remember that the colleges in highest demand do not need to advertise heavily!

Students should open a careers file and keep all the relevant information in it.

Open days are held from September on. Some schools organise trips to visit colleges. It is possible to get a list of the main open days from the Institute of Guidance Counsellors in September each year. Some of the major open days or information days are:

◆ The Higher Options Conference in late-September organised by the Irish Times and the Institute of Guidance Counsellors. Most Irish colleges and many U.K. colleges attend and there is a parents' session one evening. Talks are given on different careers during the day.

◆ In February FAS, in conjunction with the Institute of Guidance Counsellors and the Irish Independent, organise a three-day seminar on careers and employment trends which includes lectures and displays.

◆ UCD runs open days in mid-March with over 20,000 students attending.

◆ DCU runs an open day on the third Saturday in November.

◆ Trinity College, NCAD and Mater Dei have open days in December.

◆ University of Limerick has an open day in January.

◆ Most of the Institutes of Technology have open days.

◆ PLC colleges hold open days during the months of February and March.

If the student or parents are interested in a particular college, ring the college and ask if there is to be an open day. Even if there is not, the staff in the various colleges often make the time available to talk to individual interested students.

Work experience can be another invaluable way to obtain information about careers. I would encourage students to look for work experience during transition year or the summers following transition year or fifth year. It can help them choose a career direction and be of positive benefit if there is an interview for the course.

Of course the key questions are: what courses will students research? What careers interests them? The answer to these questions lie in a process which begins soon after they enter second-level. Some of the constituent factors in making the decision are:

◆ Ability. Each student has different profiles of ability. A test used very much in Irish Schools is DATS (Differential Aptitude Testing) which gives a percentile score based on national norms of a student's ability in Verbal Reasoning, Numeric Reasoning, Abstract Reasoning, Spatial Relations, Mechanical Reasoning, Clerical Speed and Accuracy, Spelling and Grammar. In the case of students with dyslexia psychological assessments provide much more detailed information on the student's ability and should help the student focus on certain careers and avoid others. These assessments could be even more relevant than the DATS. If the student's profile either from DATS or a psychological assessment has particular strengths and weaknesses, career choices should be centred on the strengths. The student with difficulties in spelling and verbal expression would be wise to avoid careers where verbal skills are important such as office work or journalism. It appears to be a pattern that some students with dyslexia have a strength in spatial relations. This could lead into art, architecture, engineering or design.

◆ Achievement. Achievement is different from ability. Some students with seemingly low levels of ability can achieve very good results if they have perseverance and motivation to focus on their studies. Other students with excellent ability can do quite badly. A pattern of achievement will be built up by monitoring school reports. Expectations of results in state exams can be based on this. It is highly unlikely that a student who is achieving the grades of 'E' and 'D' during fifth and sixth year will jump to grades of 'A' and 'B' in the Leaving

Certificate examination. For most students their grades will be close to their level of achievement in school. This makes it possible to predict the probable range of results in state examinations that a student may achieve. This information can form part of the career decision and helps to make the choice realistic. If a student's results in house exams are around 250 points, the estimated range of the Leaving Certificate results could be between 200 to 350. It is realistic for the student to ensure courses in this range are included on the CAO application. In the CAO system where there are twenty choices (fifty if nursing is included) to be made, the student may still use some of those choices for courses that may go for 400 plus points but he should also ensure he has courses in the range of 200 points.

- Interest Testing. These are tests which ask the students questions about careers and indicate their level of interest in different careers groups. These tests are often used at the stage of option choice for senior cycle. In recent years computerised interest tests have become more common. *Career Directions* and *CareersWorld* are two such tests. CareersWorld is available on the internet at www.careersworld.com.

- Included in some of the interest testing can be questions about the students' interests and personality such as: What do they like to do with their spare time? Do they like to work as part of a team? Do they enjoy organising events? Would they prefer to spend their time mending machines or playing sports or board games? Do they like activities that help care for people such as First Aid or visiting elderly relatives?

- Other achievements outside the academic: Have they been involved in sports teams, First Aid, in drama, in life-saving, in sailing or music? How proficient are they in these activities? Do they want this activity to continue as part of their career? Do they have a driving licence? Sometimes leisure interests and achievements provide a route to a career choice.

- Work experience will also give students ideas about the type of work they would like to pursue or avoid in the future. It will also provide them with a reference which may be useful at interviews later on.

All these threads; achievement, ability, interests, personality, work experience and other non-academic achievement, form a realistic basis to the process of career decision. It should also provide a list of possible career directions that the student would like to research further. Once the student begins to research the courses available and different routes to qualifications, his ideas will be further refined. It is a process that will take time and should be ongoing during all of senior cycle. Preferably it will have started sooner.

Occasionally students will present in sixth year as having no idea as to what career interests them. This can provide a serious obstacle to a discussion. However, if presented with a list of broad career groupings, many of these students have very clear ideas about careers they do **not** want to pursue and it is possible to reduce the list to maybe six broad career headings which they might consider. This provides a good starting point for research.

The above discussion on career choice focuses on the individual's aptitudes, interests and achievements. Another factor to consider is the employment trends. These are notoriously unpredictable. This is because of the changing nature of jobs due to technology and the global market. There are many jobs being advertised now which were not in existence ten years ago. However there are some patterns discernible:

- ◆ The employment growth which took place during the 1990's has provided opportunities for school-leavers. The students who will benefit most will the students with qualifications and/or good skills.

- ◆ Certain sectors of the economy are providing major employment prospects. In 1998 the Government set up the Expert Group on Future Skills Needs, www.skillsireland.ie. This website is intended to be the most comprehensive source of all research on labour and skills issues in Ireland. The group have identified a number of key occupation/skills areas which are expected to experience skills shortages over the coming years. These include:

- Computer and electronics.
- Science such as Physicist, Biochemist, etc.
- Food science and technology.
- Town Planning.
- Construction craftspeople.
- Manufacturing technology.
- Engineering of all types.
- Telecommunications.

◆ There is going to be more contract work and fewer permanent appointments. The economy that now exists in Ireland provides the encouraging environment for qualified and skilled workers to set up their own businesses. This is an increasingly attractive option given the growing impermanence of employment.

◆ Because of the developments in technology and resulting changes in job practices, there is a great need for adaptability and flexibility. Workers will need to constantly up-date their skills and information.

Up-to-date information on career trends appears in the newspapers usually in August and January, both critical times for course choices. The FAS seminar in February discusses trends in employment. It makes sense that information on employment trends would be part of a decision on career direction.

List of Post Leaving Certificate Colleges

A

This list includes the main PLC colleges. Further information is available from the Vocational Education Committees in each county.

Dublin

Ballsbridge College of Further Education, www.ballsbridgecollege.com
01-6684806

Ballyfermot College of Further Education, www.bcfe.ie 01-6269421

St. Kevin's College, 01-4536397

Colaiste Dhulaigh, Coolock, www.colaistedhulaigh.ie 01-8474399

Crumlin College of Further Education, www.iol.ie/~crumlin
01-4540662

Colaiste Ide, College of Further Education, Finglas, 01-8342333

Inchicore College of Further Education, 01-4535358

Killester College, 01-8337686

Kylemore College, Dublin 10 01-6265901

Liberties College, Dublin 8, 01-4540082

Marino College, Dublin 3, 01-8334201

Pearse College, Crumlin www.pearsecollege.cdvec.ie 01-4536661

Plunkett College, Whitehall, 01-8371689

Rathmines Senior College, 01-4975334

Ringsend Technical Institute, http://indigo.ie/~ringtec/ 01-6684498

Whitehall House College of Further Education, 1-8376011

College of Further Education, Dundrum, www.cfedundrum.com
01-2985412

Dundrum College, 01-2982340

Stillorgan Senior College, 01-2880704

Dun Laoghaire Senior College, 01-2800385
Dun Laoghaire College of Further Education, www.dlcfe.ie
   01-2809676
Greenhills College, 01-4507779
Sallynoggin Senior College of Further Education, www.scs.dife.ie
   01-2852997

Cavan
Cavan College of Further Studies, www.ccfs.ie 049-4332633

Carlow
Carlow Institute of Further Education, 0503-31187

Cork
Scoil Stiofain Naofa, College of Further Education,021-4961020
St. John's Central College, www.stjohnscollege.com 021-4276410
Cork College of Commerce, 021-4270777

Donegal
Letterkenny Vocational School, 074-21047

Galway
Community College, Moinin na gCiseach, www.cgvec.ie
   091-755464
Galway Technical Institute, www.cgvec.ie 091-581342

Kerry
Tralee Community School, www.ncte.ie/traleecc 066-7121741

Kildare
Kildare College of Further Studies, 045-521287

Kilkenny
Ormond College, Kilkenny, 056-221108
Greenan College, Thomastown, 056-24112

Laois
Portlaoise Senior College, 0502-21480

Limerick
Limerick Senior College, 061-414344

Louth
Drogheda College of Further Education, 041-9837105
O Fiaich College, Dundalk, www.homepage.tinet.ie/~fiaich
042-9331398

Monaghan
Monaghan Institute of Further Education, 047-84900

Sligo
Ballinode College, 071-45480

Tipperary
Central Technical Institute, Clonmel, www.cti-clonmel.ie 052-21450

Waterford
Central Technical Institute, 051-874053
Dungarvan Technical College, 058-41184

Westmeath
Moate Business College, 0902-81178

Wexford
Enniscorthy Vocational College. 054-34185

Wicklow
Bray Institute of Further Education, www.bife.ie 01-2866233

The Dyslexia Association of Ireland

The Dyslexia Association of Ireland is a voluntary organisation and a charity. It aims to increase awareness of specific learning disability and promote the welfare of people with dyslexia.

The Association has lobbied for thirty years for the recognition of dyslexia as a major learning difficulty. It has sought the provision of appropriate services by the State for all people with dyslexia. Currently it provides a free public information service and offers psycho-educational assessment to adults and children. It arranges group and individual tuition for children and adults and runs a full-time course for adults in conjunction with FAS. It delivers in-service courses to teachers, speakers to school and parent groups and organises seminars and conferences.

The Association has thirty-four branches, each of which runs group classes for students with dyslexia after school hours. Branches provide local parent support and awareness raising. The Association monitors and evaluates new information and teaching methods for the remediation of specific learning difficulty. It keeps in touch with relevant government departments, professional bodies and educational organisations and represents the views of its members through submissions to government on educational policy.

DAI is a founder member of the European Dyslexia Association and Spectrum, an umbrella group of associations for people with hidden learning difficulties. It has long been a corporate member of the British Dyslexia Association, a member of the Disability Federation of Ireland and the National Adult Literacy Association.

Website: www.dyslexia.ie

Appendix C

National University of Ireland

POLICY STATEMENT ON MATRICULATION REQUIREMENTS FOR STUDENTS WITH LEARNING DISABILITIES AFFECTING LANGUAGE ACQUISITION.

1. The National University of Ireland with its Constituent Universities in Dublin, Cork, Galway and Maynooth is committed to a policy of inclusivity in relation to the admission to the university of students with disabilities and recognises the achievements of the growing numbers of students with disabilities in the university. The NUI has reviewed its matriculation requirements with a view to ensuring that students with certain certifiable learning disabilities, but who in all other respects have the capacity to succeed in higher education, are not excluded from matriculation.

2. The standard matriculation requirements of the National University of Ireland are set out in an annual publication *Minimum Academic Entry and Registration (Matriculation) Requirements.* The NUI recognises that for students with learning difficulties affecting language acquisition, but who in all other respects have the capacity to succeed in higher education, these matriculation requirements may pose particular problems. Attention is drawn to the two special provisions in the current regulations which relate to students with such learning difficulties, as follows:-

   ◆ Regulation 6.2 (v) permits candidates who have been exempted from Irish at second-level to claim exemption from Irish for matriculation registration purposes. Such exemptions are granted by the NUI on the basis of the Certificates of Exemption from Irish issued by the

Department of Education in accordance with Circular M10/94.

◆ Regulation 7 provides a special route to matriculation for students who are professionally certified as having a serious hearing impairment. In such cases, students are exempt from the third language requirement and are permitted to matriculate in six subjects accepted for matriculation purposes, to include Irish or English.

3. The NUI is also prepared to consider applications seeking exemption from the third language requirement from students who are certified by a qualified professional as having a serious dyslexic condition. Such applications are considered on an individual basis. The NUI have been influenced by the Association for Higher Education Access and Disability (AHEAD) in accepting the following definition of dyslexia:-

◆ Dyslexia is one of several distinct learning disabilities. It s a specific language-based disorder of constitutional origin characterised by difficulties in single word decoding, usually reflecting insufficient phonological processing. These difficulties in single word decoding are often unexpected in relation to age and other cognitive abilities; they are not the result of generalised development disability or sensory impairment. Dyslexia is manifest by variable difficulty with different forms of language, often including, in addition to problems with reading, a conspicuous problem with acquiring proficiency in writing and spelling.

4. The NUI appreciates that for students aspiring to study at a Constituent University of the National University of Ireland, the matriculation requirements of the university will be a factor in their choice of subjects for the Leaving Certificate. Accordingly, applications for exemption from Irish and/or the third language requirement may be presented to the NUI at any stage following the completion of the Junior Certificate. Applications must be accompanied by a Schools Record Form completed by the Head of School attended. These forms are available from the National University of Ireland, 49 Merrion Square, Dublin 2. Tel: 01-6767246.

The NUI emphasises that fulfilling minimum entry requirements is just one step towards registration. Students should also familiarise themselves with the admission requirements of the university to which they intend to apply for admission.

CHANGE TO MATRICULATION REQUIREMENTS DECEMBER 2001

The NUI matriculation regulations booklet sets out the University's minimum academic requirements for students seeking to enter the constituent universities and recognised colleges of NUI. It details the circumstances in which students may be exempted from particular requirements for matriculation, such as the Irish language requirement or the third language requirement, in order to qualify for matriculation. The University is also prepared to consider applications for matriculation from students **whose circumstances are exceptional**, but are not specifically covered by the matriculation regulations. Such applications are considered on an individual basis, and should be accompanied by a School Record Form completed by the Head of School attended and where appropriate, relevant professional certification.

A student who has been allowed exemption from the study of Irish at school, on the basis of specific learning disability, in accordance with Rule 46 c (i) of the 'Rules and Programme for Secondary Schools' will qualify for exemption from the NUI Irish language and Third Language requirements for matriculation. To apply for such an exemption, a student should submit the Certificate of Exemption together with a completed School Record Form.

Further Resources

BOOKS

	Career Choice 2002, published by Level 3 Publishing and Design, 15 Pembroke St., Dublin 2
Chinn, S. & Bradley, L.	*Mathematics for Dyslexia, A Teaching Handbook* Whurr, 1993
Dyslexia Association of Ireland	*All Children learn differently, a Guide to Dyslexia* Booklet available free. Send SAE (A4 size) Postage 92c. DAI, 1 Suffolk Street, Dublin 2. *Survey on the School System and Dyslexia* 1 to cover postage and copying.
Duddy J. and R. Keane	*The Student Yearbook and Career Directory* The Student Yearbook Ltd, Shancroft, O'Hanlon Lane, Malahide
Dunne, R.	*Applying to College in 2002* Undergraduate Publications Ltd., Rock Cross, Co. Cavan
Gilroy, D.E. and T.R. Miles	*Dyslexia at College* Routledge, 1996
Hornsby, Dr. B.	*Overcoming Dyslexia* Optima, 1984

Ott, P.   *How to detect and manage Dyslexia*
Heinemann 1997

Pollock, J. and E. Waller   *Day-to-day Dyslexia in the Classroom*
Routledge, 1994

Pumfrey, P. and R. Reason   *Specific Learning Difficulty (Dyslexia) Challenges and Responses*
Routledge 1991

Stordy, B.J., Nicholl, M.J.   *The LCP Solution: The remarkable nutritional Treatment for dyslexia*
Ballantine Press

West, T.G.   *In the Mind's Eye*
Prometheus Books, 1991

VIDEOS

The Channel 4 Dyslexia video   Produced by Poseidon Film Production
Distributed by Hopeline Video
P.O. Box 515 London SW15 6LQ

How difficult can this be?
Understanding Learning
Difficulties   Eagle Hill Training Outreach
Greenwick, Connecticut. USA

Lost for Wurds   QED Programme
produced by BBC Education Section

Understanding Dyslexia   The Dyslexia Institute,
133 Gresham Road, Staines,
Middlesex TW18 2AJ

USEFUL WEB ADDRESSES

www.ahead.ie   Association for Higher Education Access and Disability

www.becta.org.uk   British Educational Communications and Technology Agency

www.bda-dyslexia.org.uk	British Dyslexia Association
www.brainwise.co.uk	Educational Kinesiology
www.careersworld.com	Careers, Mindmaps & Interest Tests
www.dyslexia.ie	Dyslexia Association of Ireland
www.education.ie	Department of Education and Science
www.homeworktips.about.com	Study plans
www.inpp.org.uk	Neuro-Physiological Theory
www.ncte.ie	National Centre for Technology in Education
www.primarymovement.org	Primary Movement
www.scoilnet.ie	Websites for schools, information on careers.
www.skillsireland.ie	Expert Group on Future Skills Needs
www.skoool.ie	Study notes for school subjects.

Useful Addresses

AHEAD, 86 St. Stephen's Green, Dublin 2.

DAI, Dyslexia Association of Ireland, Suffolk Chambers, Suffolk Street, Dublin 1.

An Bord Altranais, 31-32 Fitzwilliam Street, Dublin 2.

The British Council, 22 Mount Street, Dublin 2.

The British Dyslexia Association, 98 London Road, Reading, Berks RG1 5AU

CAO, Central Admissions Office, Tower House, Eglington Street, Galway.

CERT, CERT House, Amiens Street, Dublin 1.

The Dyslexia Computer Resource Centre, Department of Psychology, University of Hull, Hull HU6 7RX

ETC Consult, 17 Leeson Park, Dublin 6.

Gaisce, The President's Award, Block H, Dublin Castle, Dublin 2.

National Training and Development Institute, Roslyn Park, Beach Road, Sandymount, Dublin 4.

SKILL, 336 Brixton Road, London L 2W9 7AA.

Teagasc, 19 Sandymount Avenue, Dublin 4.

UCAS, Fulton House, Jessop Avenue, Cheltenham, Glouchestershire, GLE 503 35H

Youth Information Offices in local areas.

Index